T0214296

Lecture Notes in Artificial Intelligence 12381

Subseries of Lecture Notes in Computer Science

More information about this series at http://www.springer.com/series/1244

Tobias Ahlbrecht · Jürgen Dix ·
Niklas Fiekas · Tabajara Krausburg (Eds.)

The Multi-Agent Programming Contest 2019

Agents Assemble – Block by Block to Victory

 Springer

Editors
Tobias Ahlbrecht (iD)
TU Clausthal
Clausthal-Zellerfeld, Germany

Jürgen Dix (iD)
TU Clausthal
Clausthal-Zellerfeld, Germany

Niklas Fiekas (iD)
TU Clausthal
Clausthal-Zellerfeld, Germany

Tabajara Krausburg (iD)
TU Clausthal
Clausthal-Zellerfeld, Germany

ISSN 0302-9743   ISSN 1611-3349   (electronic)
Lecture Notes in Artificial Intelligence
ISBN 978-3-030-59298-1   ISBN 978-3-030-59299-8   (eBook)
https://doi.org/10.1007/978-3-030-59299-8

LNCS Sublibrary: SL7 – Artificial Intelligence

This Springer imprint is published by the registered company Springer Nature Switzerland AG
The registered company address is: Gewerbestrasse 11, 6330 Cham, Switzerland

Preface

In this volume, we present the 14th edition of the annual Multi-Agent Programming Contest (MAPC) and its participants.

The brand-new 2019 scenario is described in the first contribution, together with a brief overview of the four participating teams and their solutions. Additionally, we take a closer look at how the contest scenario has evolved over the years.

After this introduction, each agent team of the MAPC 2019 is introduced by its creators, who deliver detailed descriptions and analysis of their performance, reporting on their experience with agent technology.

Each paper passed the single-blind review process conducted by at least three reviewers per contribution.

August 2020

Tobias Ahlbrecht
Jürgen Dix
Niklas Fiekas
Tabajara Krausburg

Organization

Program Chairs

Tobias Ahlbrecht   TU Clausthal, Germany
Jürgen Dix   TU Clausthal, Germany
Niklas Fiekas   TU Clausthal, Germany
Jomi Hubner   Federal University of Santa Catarina, Brazil
Tabajara Krausburg   TU Clausthal, Germany

Program Committee

Lars Braubach   Universität Hamburg, Germany
Rem Collier   University College Dublin, Ireland
Axel Heßler   DAI-Labor, TU Berlin, Germany
Brian Logan   University of Nottingham, UK
Peter Novak   Meandair B.V., The Netherlands
Alessandro Ricci   Università di Bologna, Italy
Evangelos Sarmas   Independent, Greece
Federico Schlesinger   Zalando SE, Germany
Jaime Sichman   University of São Paulo, Brazil
Neil Yorke-Smith   TU Delft, The Netherlands
Maicon Rafael Zatelli   Federal University of Santa Catarina, Brazil

Contents

Overview

The Multi-Agent Programming Contest: A Résumé
Comparing Agent Systems 2005–2019

Tobias Ahlbrecht[1]([envelope]) [ORCID], Jürgen Dix[1] [ORCID], Niklas Fiekas[1] [ORCID],
and Tabajara Krausburg[1,2] [ORCID]

[1] Department of Informatics, Clausthal University of Technology,
Clausthal-Zellerfeld, Germany
{tobias.ahlbrecht,dix,niklas.fiekas}@tu-clausthal.de
[2] School of Technology, Pontifical Catholic University of Rio Grande do Sul,
Porto Alegre, Brazil
tabajara.rodrigues@edu.pucrs.br

Abstract. The Multi-Agent Programming Contest, MAPC, is an annual event organized since 2005 out of Clausthal University of Technology. Its aim is to investigate the potential of using decentralized, autonomously acting intelligent agents, by providing a complex scenario to be solved in a competitive environment. For this we need suitable benchmarks where agent-based systems can shine. We present previous editions of the contest and also its current scenario and results from its use in the 2019 MAPCwith a special focus on its suitability. We conclude with lessons learned over the years.

Keywords: Multi-agent systems · Decentralized computing · Cooperation · Artificial intelligence · Simulation platforms

1 Introduction

The original aim of our contest, back in the humble beginnings in 2005, was to provide a platform for comparing and evaluating systems based on *computational logic*, mainly developed for knowledge representation purposes.

We wanted to develop an interesting yet simple, but non-trivial, scenario for testing systems based on different paradigms. At that time, many knowledge-based approaches were developed as smallish PhD projects: a prototype was implemented but never seriously compared against other such systems.

Emphasis was put on the *evaluation* and *comparison* of systems, not on finding an optimal solution of a particular scenario. The creation of a scenario was always driven by the need to determine the features that a system should possess for successfully solving a complicated task. We never wanted to honor a smart idea for a solution, but the features and technology that help to tackle the problem at hand.

© Springer Nature Switzerland AG 2020
T. Ahlbrecht et al. (Eds.): MAPC 2019, LNAI 12381, pp. 3–27, 2020.
https://doi.org/10.1007/978-3-030-59299-8_1

1.1 Structure of This Work

We start with a short introduction on agent programming and the Multi-Agent Programming Contest in general. In Sect. 2, we introduce the simulation platform, followed by the history of the Contest in Sect. 3. Afterwards, we present the newest scenario and the results of the MAPC2019 in Sect. 4. We conclude with lessons learned during the contest in general and in the latest installment in particular. Throughout the article, we focus especially on the scenario aspect of the MAPC.

1.2 Agents

During the years, the systems we compared turned more and more into those based on *agent programming languages* [9] or genuine multi-agent systems (MAS) implemented in classical programming languages. The scenarios became more complex with an increasing number of agents needed to solve the task.

In contrast to many other contests, several decisions have been taken a priori:

- not to impose any restrictions on the software used;
- not to find or compare *tricky algorithms* to solve the scenario, rather we wanted to evaluate the capabilities of the system to express and model suitable constructs for dealing with the scenario;
- not to consider the perfect implementation or high performance of a system; in particular, we never considered real-time aspects, which are important for e.g. computer games.

The last bullet above reflects the situation in agent programming for many years (still today, but to a lesser extent): agent languages are still not on par with classical programming languages in terms of their efficient implementation and their maturity concerning software engineering aspects. We therefore decided to refrain from this particular aspect.

In our MAPC, each participating team develops a group of agents (during the 5–7 months between the announcement of the scenario and the contest), which remotely connect to our MAPCserver where the scenario is being run. The MAPCserver sends the current game state in the form of percepts to each agent and expects an executable action in return. The gathered actions are executed and the game state is advanced. This cycle is repeated until a predefined number of steps is reached. The remote nature of the contest also keeps the responsibility of running the agents with the participants.

The available time for each simulation step must include the latency of the internet and is, intentionally, chosen to be quite high (4 seconds): we do not consider high performance nor real-time constraints.

In addition, we have no control of the communication within a team (e.g., shared memory or not, decentralized or not). Consequently, we could not directly enforce decentralized approaches—only by designing the scenario in a way that favors them.

We also never excluded classical (i.e., non-agent) programming languages and frameworks from being used. In fact, we almost always had non-agent entries taking part in our contest and some performed very well. Obviously, one can use a classical programming language and implement certain agent-techniques that are suitable for the scenario (or use agent technology without leveraging its potential, in effect, using it like a conventional programming approach).

1.3   Goals and Purpose of the MAPC

The purpose of the contest is twofold:

1. to find out for which applications agent-oriented features pay off, as opposed to features available in classical programming languages; and
2. to compare and test the versatility and suitability of agent languages or platforms.

To answer the first question, we are developing and evolving scenarios building on the experiences from previous editions of the MAPC. By improving the scenarios, we simultaneously improve our ability to answer the second question.

However, it should be clarified that *we do not want to compare problem solutions*, instead we want to compare agent languages among themselves and against classical programming languages.

The difference between agents and classical, more centralized paradigms is, to a great deal, autonomy, communication, cooperation and to strike a good balance between proactiveness and reactiveness. Clearly, any (new) feature can be implemented in any (Turing-complete) programming language, but one would hope an agent language to be more versatile and efficient or offering built-in features for elegantly programming a solution.

Therefore we always try to develop our scenarios in such a way, that no smart solution will be sufficient, but instead the *interplay of various acting entities and their emerging features* counts.

In the end, we are especially interested in:

1. which technologies the teams used;
2. to which degree they were used (i.e., how difficult (or easy) it was to use agent-based features); and
3. which aspects were especially straightforward or challenging to design and implement.

To summarize again, the contest is an attempt to shed some light on these questions: when and to what extent do agent-oriented features pay off? Is there a particular complexity of the problem that makes these approaches beneficial? Or not at all? And how are these features supported by existing agent frameworks? We refer back to all of these questions in Sect. 5.

Last but not least, it almost comes naturally that we aim to support educational efforts in the design and implementation of agent systems by providing each year a ready, off-the-shelf package: this is a ready for action tool in the classroom and could be (and has been) used in a course on agent systems of any level. We noticed in our experience that the competition idea is especially attractive for students and results in a very engaging work atmosphere.

1.4   Related Work

Many similar competitions have been and are still being held, while most do not explicitly focus on multi-agent systems. We discuss some of them that are related to MAPCand are still active nowadays.

Directly involving agents, the *(Power) Trading Agent Competition*[1] [16] provides a trading-related scenario in the energy market. However, each team only consists of a single "broker" agent, requiring no cooperation or coordination. The goal here is to see how agents can autonomously solve supply-chain problems.

Probably the best-known are the various *RoboCup Simulation Leagues*[2]. RoboCup ranges over a variety of different domains like soccer, disaster response, and industrial logistics. Each league focuses on a specific problem that must be addressed by competitors. For instance, in RoboCupRescue two major leagues are organized on: (i) robots; and (ii) agent simulation. The first centers around (virtual) robots and less around abstract agents. For example, agents have noisy virtual sensors or may be subjected to complex physics, focusing on realism. The agent simulation league provides virtual agents placed on a map of a city that has been damaged by an earthquake event. Competitors focus on different self-isolated AI problems (e.g., task allocation) provided by the contest [18]. In addition, all teams have to give a presentation on their solution, which counts towards their final score.

There is also a number of challenges targeting specific problem domains, e.g. the *International Planning Competition* [17]. Here, of course planning is in the limelight, while in our contest it is only one possible component of an agent team. At the other end, the *General Game Playing* [12] competitions do not focus on one particular feature but on the ability of general AI systems to play an arbitrary game upon receiving its rules.

Finally, there are more than a few challenges focusing on finding (autonomous) solutions for existing commercial games, like the *Mario AI Championship*[3] [15] or the *Student StarCraft AI tournament*[4], or specifically designed games like *BattleCode*[5]. The goal here is usually to benchmark game AI techniques and algorithms.

We would also like to mention a new challenge, the Intention Progression Competition[6], which focuses on a specific issue within agent systems: the Intention Progression Problem, i.e. the decision of agents about how to proceed with

---

[1] www.powertac.org.
[2] www.robocup.org.
[3] www.marioai.org.
[4] www.sscaitournament.com.
[5] www.battlecode.org.
[6] www.intentionprogression.org.

their given intentions and plans in order to reach their goals. Thus, a solution for the MAPC(e.g. an agent) could be seen as a specific input challenge in the IPC, while solutions for the IPC could be used in agent platforms that participate in the MAPC.

Not a competition but definitely worth mentioning is the Blocks World for Teams (BW4T) [14] environment, which is not quite unlike the current MAPCscenario. There, agents have to coordinate to deliver sequences of color-coded blocks.

2   The MASSim Framework

The first edition of the MAPCin 2005 presented a simple scenario description that had to be implemented in its totality by each participant and delivered as an executable.

2.1   From 2006: The Early Days

In 2006, the *MASSim* platform was introduced: an extensible simulation server written in Java that provides the environment facilities. Agent programs can connect through the network to a *MASSim* server while agents run in the competitors' own computer infrastructure.

Since then, the format of the MAPChas been that of two teams competing against each other for performance in each simulation, and the overall winner of the contest defined by summing up the points after all participants have competed in simulations against each other, in a regular sports tournament fashion.

All simulations are run in a discrete step-by-step manner. In each step all agents execute their actions simultaneously from the point of view of the server, and there is a time limit within which agents must choose an action (otherwise they are regarded as a no-op). In the beginning of each step's cycle, the server sends each agent their current percepts of the environment, and waits for the response that specifies the action to execute.

When the responses from all agents are received or when the timeout limit is reached, all received actions are executed in *MASSim*. The actions (mostly) have an immediate effect on the environment and the new state of the simulation is computed which results in new agent percepts for the next simulation step.

This cycle is repeated for a fixed number of steps, and then a winner is decided according to scenario-specific criteria (usually having achieved the highest score).

MASSim is fully implemented in Java, and the information exchange with the agent programs is realized through XML messages. These messages can also be accessed as ready percept objects through the EISMASSim interface layer, which is explained later.

2.2   2017 Until Today: Simply Going Forward

In early 2017, *MASSim* was completely rewritten. XML messages were removed in favor of the more efficient JSON format.

We switched from having both a Java RMI based monitor and a web monitor to a single web-based monitor.

Also, we abandoned the former plug-in architecture in favor of an annual package, which helped in keeping the package small and freed us of having to keep *MASSim* backwards-compatible to all previous scenarios.[7]

This rewrite also allowed us to create a platform with more than two concurrent teams in mind. While we have not used this yet, it remains a tempting option for future scenarios.

Figure 1 displays the current architecture. Boxes are components, while regular arrows depict that a component uses another.

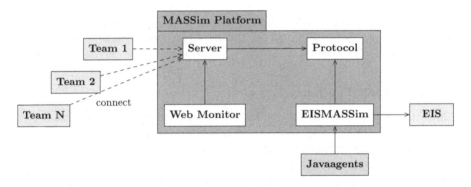

Fig. 1. The *MASSim* architecture.

The server package is responsible for running the simulations and handling connections to all agents. It only uses the facilities of the protocol package to build percept messages for agents and parse action messages it receives.

The classes used to build valid messages according to the protocol have been extracted into a self-contained protocol package that helps both with parsing JSON data into Java objects and transforming Java message objects into their JSON representation. Thus, it is e.g. used by the server to create messages for all agents. The protocol is also used by the EISMASSim component, which can be used by agent platforms to connect to the server. This component handles the whole login procedure and then translates perception and action messages into actions and percepts according to the EIS (Environment Interface Standard [7]) and vice versa. In the terms of EIS, EISMASSim is what makes *MASSim* an "EIS-enabled" environment. That is, all agent platforms that support EIS can connect to the *MASSim* server without any additional effort (though sometimes there are still some initial difficulties).

We also provide a sample implementation of agents using EISMASSim in the `Javaagents` package. Participants using Java-based platforms may connect to the server by integrating EISMASSim, using the protocol package, or, just as non-Java-teams, parse and build their own JSON messages according to the protocol.

---

[7] You can still play the old releases using their respective packages.

Finally, the web monitor is started by the server if requested and then retrieves the current game state from the server after each step.

The current *MASSim* package is fully open-source and openly available (https://multi-agentcontest.org/2019). It is not only used for the MAPC, but has also proved useful both for researchers testing their advancements in the field, and in the classroom, aiding the teaching of the multi-agent programming paradigm (https://multi-agentcontest.org/massim-in-teaching).

3   History and Evolution of the Contest

We can roughly divide the contest into two phases. In the early phase, there was not much cooperation among the agents: they acted more or less on their own. This led us to reconsider our scenario and we ended up with the *Agents on Mars* scenario, where we experienced some really interesting games. This then evolved into the *Agents in the City* (or simply *City*) scenario, which was even more realistic as it considered agents acting in a real city using actual city maps. We then adapted the *City* scenario, removing some of its complexity (regarding implementation effort for the participants) and incorporating features we think were interesting from previous scenarios, which led to the *Agents Assemble* scenario, which we will present and analyze in detail in Sect. 4.

3.1   Early Phase

The scenario used for the first edition of the MAPC(2005) consisted of a simple grid in which agents could move to empty adjacent spaces. Food units would appear randomly through the simulation, and the objective was to collect these units and carry them to a storage location.

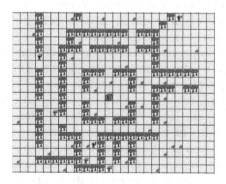

Fig. 2. The Gold Miners scenario.

The idea was refined for the second edition [6]: *Gold Miners* (Fig. 2). Now the agents were to collect gold in a competitive environment against another team, and some obstacles were introduced to the grid to add some navigation complexity. This scenario, which was also used in the third edition of the contest, was still very simplistic, and in the proposed solutions agents acted independently of their teammates: no cooperation or coordinated behavior took place.

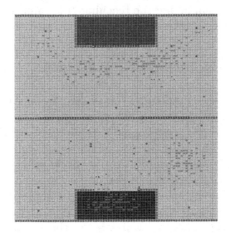

Fig. 3. The Cows and Cowboys scenario.

For the 2008–2010 editions [6], a new scenario was designed that *demands* coordination from agents: *Cows and Cowboys*, as shown in Fig. 3. Still using a grid as the underlying map, the goal for this scenario was to lead a group of cows to a particular area of the map, the team's own "corral", while preventing the opponent team from doing the same. The cows were animated entities that reacted to the agents' positions by trying to avoid them. Solving the map required agents to coordinate their positions in order to lead big groups of cows into the corrals, whereas a single agent would in most cases disperse the group of cows and fail to lead them in the desired direction.

Even in this clearly cooperative scenario, one team found a way of letting each agent work independently, always pushing a single cow. This team promptly won the contest (though out-of-competition) and we learned that *features we want to see need to be enforced rather than rewarded*, since participating teams always tend to find (and go for) the path of least resistance. Thus, a flocking algorithm for cows was introduced, which made the cows form groups and avoid agents more strongly. This allowed good teams to capture entire herds with the right agent formations, while single agents could not achieve anything anymore. In addition, fences were added as another cooperative element: agents had to stand on switches to open them and communicate to get all agents and cows safely through. In that way we achieved some cooperation among agents and saw even more interesting games.

3.2 Agents on Mars

The *Agents on Mars* scenario [5] was used from 2011–2014. It turned out to be an important step in the contest's evolution, as it introduced many innovative features and increased the game's complexity. The map took the form of a weighted graph representing the surface of the planet Mars (we always based the scenario on a fictitious story). The agents represent *All Terrain Vehicles* of different kinds, and their goal in the game is to discover the best water wells by exploring the map and then to keep control of as many wells as possible. This was done by placing themselves in specific formations that ensure a covering of an area containing the wells while keeping rival agents outside.

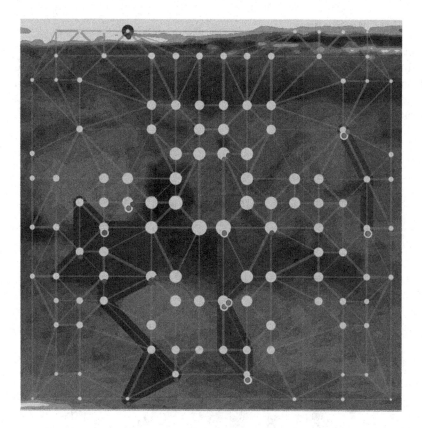

Fig. 4. The "Agents on Mars" scenario. (Color figure online)

In Fig. 4, one can see the basic graph layout, where the node sizes represent their value. The small circles at some nodes are the agents and the colored parts of the graph are currently taken by the team of the respective color.

The new agents were much more complex entities than in the previous scenarios: they had a rich set of actions to choose from, in contrast to just moving around the map. Furthermore, they dealt with a set of internal parameters that could vary through the simulation—*Energy*, *Visibility Range*, *Health* and *Strength*.

The evolution in the complexity of the scenario has remained on par with the evolution of multi-agent programming technologies used by the participating teams. A good quality of the teams has been reached and resulted in interesting games. Unlike previous scenarios, a (simple) strategy that works against each and every rival has not been discovered. However, it became difficult to further evolve the scenario. Also, it was a rather abstract problem.

3.3   The City Scenario

Our previous scenario, pictured in Fig. 5, was first used in 2016 [2] and improved two times for the editions of 2017 [3] and 2018 [4]. We started with two teams of 16 agents each moving through the streets of a digital city backed by realistic street graph data from *OpenStreetMap*[8]. The number of agents was then increased to 28 and 34 per team respectively.

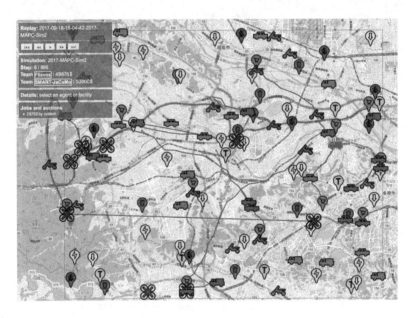

Fig. 5. The "Agents in the City" scenario.

Each team's goal was simply to earn as much money as possible by completing randomly generated jobs. These jobs required the agents to move around the

---
[8] https://www.openstreetmap.org.

city, buy certain kinds of items, cooperatively assemble these items to get new item types and finally deliver the finished products to a predefined target location. Most of these jobs were available for both agent teams simultaneously and rewarded on a *first come, first served* basis, allowing for more direct competition.

Each agent had one of four distinct roles, which characterized its movement type (air- or road-bound) and speed, as well as its maximum battery and carrying capacity. As is tradition, the number of agents was increased for each scenario to provide a greater challenge of coordination and require some more computational effort. Different agent roles were first introduced with the *Agents-on-Mars* scenario. The roles differed by certain key attributes as well as by which action was usable by which agent.

Compared to our previous scenarios, this one required more coordination and planning among agents of the same team. Some jobs are more profitable than other co-occurring jobs. Once agents are able to identify good jobs, the real challenge is the coordination of which agent secures which items from where in order to strike a good balance between time efficiency and money spent.

For the third instance of the scenario, we added a new *well* facility that teams could build and opposing teams could dismantle. To build wells, some funds had to be spent which could again be acquired by completing jobs. The wells would then generate points for as long as they existed. This change was intended to increase interaction between the teams and make the agents' actions more visible to human observers.

Lessons Learned in the City. The first run in 2016 has shown once again that participants have to be coerced into using specific features of the scenario: for example, we had to make cooperative assembly mandatory in 2017.

For the second run in 2017, we noticed a problem with the many parameters controlling the random generation of simulation instances. Finding *good* sets of parameters was not an easy task and required considerable testing. Also, for the first time we experienced that a scenario should allow for a simple naive (but far from being optimal) solution to be quickly producible. This scenario instead required considerable agent programming work before first results could be seen.

Another downside was that the visualization did not (or could not) show everything that was going on in an easily discernible way. For example, it is very impractical to display for all agents which items they are currently transporting. To amend this a little, the wells were added in 2018 to have an element that plainly shows how well a team is doing aside from the current money value.

Also, interaction between the teams was very limited and only indirectly given through the availability of shared resources (i.e. items in the shops) and the competition to get a job done first in order to receive the reward. The wells were also added to have a new entity that agents of both teams could and needed to interact with.

4   2019: Agents Assemble

After having played the *City* scenario for three consecutive years, it was once
again time to come up with a fresh scenario and apply the lessons learned. We
wanted to address some of the issues with the previous scenario, like visibility
of agent behavior, while keeping many of the factors that made it interesting.

4.1   Scenario

In the new *Agents Assemble* scenario, as the name suggest, agents again have
to construct complex structures from base objects. We switched from the map-
(or graph-)based environment back to a "simple" grid structure with obstacles
(see Fig. 6), comparable to the *Cow* scenario. The agents have to explore the
grid to find `blocks` which also occupy one cell of the grid. Each agent has four
"arms", one to each side, which can be used to pick up or connect to blocks.
Blocks which are connected to an agent move in the same direction as the agent.
Two adjacent blocks can also be connected to each other by two agents from the
same team, when each agent is holding one of the blocks.

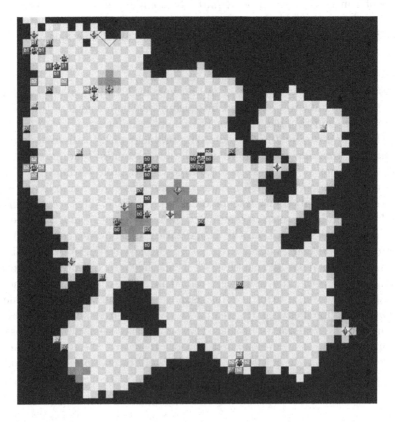

Fig. 6. MAPC2019 environment. Agents possess a local view of it and are required to
assemble complex shapes to be delivered.

The system then randomly creates **tasks**, which the agents have to complete to earn reward points. The team with the most points at the end of the simulation will be the winner. Each task basically describes a structure or formation of blocks that the agents have to create. We depict an example of tasks in Fig. 7. Once the shape is assembled, the agents can deliver it to one of the goal zones to receive the points.

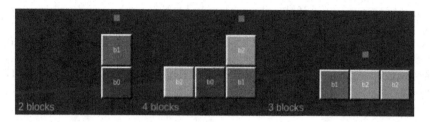

Fig. 7. Some examples of tasks in which the delivery agent should be carrying the blocks at the red dot position depicted in the figure. (Color figure online)

Actions. The agents have different actions for moving around in the grid. They can move one cell in each of the four main directions per step or rotate 90 degrees. This rotation might be handy, if the agents have blocks attached. Further, there is an action to retrieve blocks from **dispensers**, which are placed in random locations and provide one specific type of block. To work with blocks, the agents have actions for attaching and detaching things to their sides and as mentioned before, two agents can use the **connect** action to join two blocks together. An agent can also break this connection between two blocks, if the blocks are attached to the agent (directly or indirectly).

To interact with the environment and other agents, the **clear** action was added. It targets a single cell within the agent's vision radius (up to 5 cells in Manhattan distance) and has to be "charged", i.e. executed a certain number of times for the same target cell before it has an effect. Once it resolves, if the cell contained an obstacle or block, these will vanish and leave an empty cell. If instead an agent occupied that cell, it will be disabled. In that case, this agent will not be able to execute actions for a certain number of steps and also, all of its attached blocks (if any) will not be attached to the agent anymore. To give each agent a chance to avoid this, the target cells to be cleared have a perceivable marker after each **clear** action, i.e. also while charging.

As always, each action has a number of specific failure codes, indicating the reason why the action could not be executed.

Perception. One of the novelties of this scenario is that agents only perceive relative coordinates. That is, at the beginning the agents cannot know where they are. Due to their limited vision range of five cells in each direction, they do not even know where they are relative to each other and have to find their teammates first.

This might favor solutions, where a local agent perspective is taken, rather than centralized approaches.

Dynamic Environment. To give the agents an even greater challenge, the environment dynamically changes during the matches. This makes harder for the agents to remember if they have already been at a place and requires more adaptability.

During each game, a number of `clear events` will occur. These work almost exactly like the `clear` action, only they affect a bigger region of the grid and after each event, new obstacles will appear randomly distributed around the center of the event.

Blocks and Visibility. One drawback of the *City* scenario was that it was not very interesting to watch, because most of the action did not happen in the environment. When agents bought items, these just went to their inventories. The current possessions of an agent could be displayed in a list, but it was rather difficult to keep track of multiple agents at once, not to mention all of them. Thus, in the new scenario, items (i.e., `blocks`) have received a more tangible representation, taking up considerable space in the environment. This leads to more interaction between agents and items and all of it is easily observable by human bystanders. What's more, carrying assembled shapes around becomes even more of a challenge, as the number of available routes possibly decreases.

4.2   Participants

This year, we had four teams participating in the Contest.

FIT BUT. The team from Czech Brno University of Technology consists of three people and participated in the Contest for the first time. The agents are implemented in plain Java.

GOAL-DTU. The team from Technical University of Denmark has already participated in the MAPCin one form or another for many, many years and has never missed a Contest since. As the name suggests, the agents were implemented using the GOAL [13] agent language.

LFC. The team LFC, from University of Liverpool, used JaCaMo [8] to implement its agent team. An additional fast downward planning component was developed to support the agents.

TRG. The single-person team TRG from the Canadian Carleton University also participated in the Contest for the first time. The agents were implemented with the Jason [10] framework.

An overview of the teams is listed in Table 1.

As we can see, this year, all approaches involve Java at some level. *FIT BUT* uses Java directly, while *TRG* uses Jason, which is implemented in Java. JaCaMo,

Table 1. Team overview

	FIT BUT	GOAL-DTU	LFC	TRG
System	Java	GOAL	JaCaMo	Jason
Team size	3	3	3	1
Time invested (in h)	300–400	200	200	500–600
Previously participated	No	Partly	Partly	No
Lines of Code (LOC)	5500–6300	1000	6800	9700
Started	August (29th)	August	May/September	May/mid-July
Total Score	1760	330	1790	590
Points	15	10	22	5
Win/Draw/Lose	5/-/4	3/1/5	7/1/1	1/2/6
Ranking	2	3	1	4

as used by *LFC*, in turn leverages Jason for implementing the agent reasoning. Lastly, *GOAL-DTU* uses GOAL, which is also implemented in Java.

Additionally, all teams are using an approach based on or at least somehow related to the BDI model [11], where agents' knowledge is represented in terms of beliefs, agents have some desires, or goals they want to achieve, and intentions, representing what an agent has elected to do. Jason, also as part of JaCaMo, is a platform for creating BDI agents. *FIT BUT* on the other hand used Java to implement their own system inspired by the BDI model. Lastly, cognitive agents implemented in GOAL also have beliefs and desires and the concept of intention also finds (informal) representation.

The teams are of similar size, except for *TRG*. Notably though, the single-person team has invested the most time. Of the four teams, *TRG* and *FIT BUT* are completely new to the Contest, while some members of *GOAL-DTU* and *LFC* had already participated before. We also note that the GOAL solution is particularly small in terms of LOC, while the Jason-based solution is a bit larger than the average.[9]

LFC and *TRG* started their initial work in May, than letting it rest until starting for real in September and July respectively. *FIT BUT* and *GOAL-DTU* both started to work in August.

4.3 Tournament and Results

In the final tournament, each team plays one match against each other team, where one match consists of three simulations with different parameters. Thus, with four teams, each team had to play 9 games. Winning a simulation is awarded

---

[9] This does not necessarily tell us anything about GOAL or Jason though.

with three tournament points, while a draw means one point for each team. The best result a team can achieve is 27 points.

We had the teams play simulations with three different sets of parameters, so that they were less likely to optimize their systems to one particular setting. Each simulation ran for 500 steps and 10 agents per team. In the second simulation, more complex tasks, with up to 5 required blocks instead of 3, were offered. In the third simulation, we increased the chance of a random clear event happening from 4% to 8%, leading to a more uncertain environment.

The results are also listed in Table 1. The Contest was won by the JaCaMo-based solution from Liverpool's *LFC*, with only one loss against *GOAL-DTU* and one draw against *TRG* out of 9 games, resulting in 22 tournament points. Runner-up is *FIT BUT* with 15 points, while *GOAL-DTU* achieved 10 and *TRG* 5 points. We note that each team won at least one simulation, and never only because the other team failed completely. All teams presented a workable solution.

Strategies. No team found a *strategic* advantage over the others. That is, we did not see a particular strategy being used to great effect. While the agent teams approached the problem in different ways, none of these were clearly superior to all others.

The Contest winner, *LFC*, implemented a strategy, where one agent was always waiting in a goal zone for its team members to deliver exactly the blocks needed for a particular task. We saw each agent always carry at most one block at a time. The shape required for the task was always assembled together with the agent waiting in the goal zone, who then submitted the task upon its completion. One advantage of *LFC* was clearly the capability to "dig" straight lines through obstacles with repeated clear actions. This technique was also used by the agents at the start of each simulation, probably to find the actual boundaries of the grid environment (which was always surrounded by a wall of obstacles). *LFC* implemented dynamic roles, where agents would start as explorers and later switch to specializations, e.g. assembling agents waiting in the goal zones.

FIT BUT in contrast had their agents meet somewhere on their routes to connect their blocks. Thus we saw *FIT BUT* agents walking around with complex shapes attached, which also worked very well.

GOAL-DTU agents could always be recognized by them proactively requesting as much as four blocks at a time and subsequently moving with four blocks of one type attached. While this ensured that they always had enough blocks at their disposal, it made it more difficult to navigate the map, especially during the late game when clear events could have already created narrow paths.

TRG alone tried a hybrid strategy. While some agents were coordinating to complete tasks, the other agents were trying to "defend" each goal zone by using clear actions on approaching opponent agents. This was an interesting decision, which unfortunately did not pay off so well, as the agents from the other teams were mostly able to circumvent these interventions. These roles were also statically assigned and did not depend on the current situation.

While we always try to build and configure the scenario in such a way, that no single best (and maybe even simple) strategy exists, we can never be sure that we succeed in this. Generally, the more features and interactions among them a scenario has, the harder it becomes to balance all of these features "correctly", so that no single feature can be used in an unforeseen way. Thus, in the new scenario, the rules governing the simulations were kept as simple as possible.

4.4   Interesting Simulations

In this section, we want to take a look at some interesting simulations[10] to see how the teams compare to each other under similar circumstances. All replays are also accessible from the contest overview page[11].

2nd Simulation of *GOAL-DTU* vs. *LFC*. Of course this simulation[12] might be interesting since it was the only one that *LFC* lost. The final score was 130 to 40 for *GOAL-DTU*. If we look at the completed tasks, we see that *GOAL-DTU* was already able to submit a task in step 78, which yielded 90 points, since the required shape consisted of three blocks. After this however, for more than 200 steps "nothing" happens. The next task is completed, again by *GOAL-DTU*, in step 317, netting 40 points for a two-block shape. *LFC* only completes one task, in step 351, receiving the 40 points. After this, no further tasks are completed. So, one question is surely what did *LFC* do before step 351. Reviewing all other simulations of *LFC*, the agents were always able to complete their first task around step 200. In step 191, we find instead the situation depicted in Fig. 8.

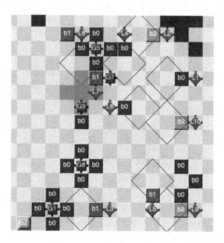

Fig. 8. Step 191: *LFC* clearing their blocks. (Color figure online)

---

[10] Not saying that some of the simulations were not interesting!.

[11] https://multiagentcontest.org/2019/.

[12] https://multiagentcontest.org/replays_2019/?2019-10-16-17-22-57-1571239377138_
GOAL-DTU_LFC.

The green *LFC* agents (diamond-shaped, labels start with an "L", located at the top and right of this clipping), are all charging a `clear` action (red diamond markers on the grid) to remove the block they have currently attached. From their usual strategy, we conclude that their plan was to attach blocks to agent L7, who was already waiting in the goal zone (the red filled diamond shaped area near the center of the image; the smaller red diamond outline marks the clear action). If we go back in time, we see that the *GOAL-DTU* agents are and have been very active in this region, carrying lots of blocks, as always. First, this makes it very difficult for *LFC* to get their blocks to the L7 agent. Secondly, the *LFC* agents decide to abandon their whole plan, even clearing all blocks they have already gathered. If we assume that *LFC* has to start anew (minus some initial discovery and exploration), we might indeed expect the next task to be completed after another 100 to 150 steps, which proved to be the case.

2nd Simulation of *LFC* vs. *TRG*. In this simulation[13] both teams were not able to score. This is quite surprising since *LFC* scored in all simulations but this one. Moreover, *LFC* was the team that scored most in the contest: 1790 points. Considering only simulations against *TRG*, it scored 180 in the first, and 210 points in the third. The question is: why did *LFC* perform much better in those other simulations?

To understand that, we need to look at *TRG*'s strategy. They always seek to position agents in the goal zone to disable any agent that enters that place. Nevertheless, it does not always work. At some times, some goal zone receives no *TRG* agents. As *LFC*'s strategy is to always choose a single goal zone to be used, at the second simulation, both strategies have collided. Every time *LFC*'s agents tried to deliver a task, a *TRG* agent was there to disable them. An example of this event is depicted in Fig. 9.

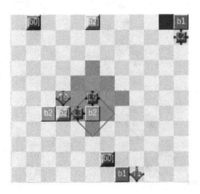

Fig. 9. The exact moment (step 174) when a *TRG* agent disables *LFC*'s agents.

---

[13] https://multiagentcontest.org/replays_2019/?2019-10-16-15-39-17-1571233157086_LFC_TRG.

This strategy seems to break the *LFC* team, because once their delivery agent is disabled, the whole team restarts to clear blocks and search for the grid's boundaries again. Whilst *LFC* is unable to deliver tasks, so is *TRG*. *TRG*'s strategy for preventing a team to score works pretty well, on the other hand, their agents were not able to coordinate themselves to form shapes required by tasks. At the end of the second simulation, no team scored a single point.

4.5   Survey Results

Traditionally, we conclude the Contest with a questionnaire that we ask each team to answer[14]. At this point, we give a brief summary of the answers from all teams. Parts of the survey results have already been used to create Table 1.

Regarding the motivation, practicing MAS development and in general learning more about agent technology were given as the main reasons for participating in the MAPC. This is aligned with MAPC's goal, in which in order to stimulate research in MAS, we need more people to learn and practice it.

We noticed that many teams mentioned that **debugging** capabilities were quite limited. Thus, they often resorted to "print(.)" as a debugging tool, i.e. adding logging statements and reading or searching the traces afterwards. Some teams stated that debugging was the most time-consuming task and some even developed their own (scenario-specific) tools that helped them to understand what was going on. Other time-consuming tasks include map navigation and merging the local views of the agents.

The most challenging aspects of the scenario according to the teams were:

- the dynamic environment;
- the local perspective of the agents; and
- coordinating agents to perform the synchronous actions.

From the survey, we also know that the teams barely added additional AI techniques to improve their solution (aside from *LFC* using a fast downward planner). This is probably due to the additional time investments required to add features to systems that are already quite complex within a limited timespan.

The main advantages of using agent technology were seen as *flexibility* and *modularity* of the system. From an agent programming perspective, agents should consider constantly the current state to select a proper action which may be a useful feature in dynamic environments. As the main drawbacks, teams cited the difficulty in debugging, a lack of portability and that it was very challenging to keep the system simple and easy to maintain.

Finally, if teams were to attend another time, they would like to improve error handling, reliability, coordination of their agents and their own debugging means.

---

[14] The reader will find these answers at the end of each team description paper.

5 Lessons Learned

The organization of our MAPCturned out to be quite work-intensive at times. Its technical implementation has been mainly done or supervised by (to this day seven) PhD students of the second author, in addition to a number of Bachelor and Master theses. However, the students also played a major role in crafting the scenarios and coming up with fresh and innovative ideas.

In the first phase of the MAPC, no real cooperation among agents was achieved. In fact *every man for himself* was a common strategy, completely against the paradigm of agent programming. Often the teams with the best working A^* path-finding algorithm won. Due to the fact that the participating agent languages were not yet mature enough, the main benefit of the contest in the early days was to serve as a debugging tool for the participating systems.

Indeed, low-level technical problems with the implementations of the agent languages often played a major role. This is in contrast to the second phase, where attention shifted to the scenario and higher-level concerns.

5.1 Agents Assemble Scenario

In the new scenario, we saw that forcing agents to work solely off their local perspectives and integrate their knowledge with other agents is a challenging task.

We once again note that it's desirable to have a problem that is easy to solve, but very difficult to solve well. In other words, it should be easy to come up with some agents that can play the game, while mastering it should require a lot of effort.

Aside from *TRG*trying to defend goal zones, we only saw limited conscious interaction between the teams. Unfortunately, our options to elicit interaction are also limited, because there is little motivation to cooperate in a zero-sum game. As such, it would only work if both teams are deceived to varying degrees. Another way would be some form of attacking, though we try to keep our scenarios as peaceful as possible. In this scenario, we had indirect interaction through presence in and modification of a shared environment, similar to the *Cow* scenario. In the *City* scenario, we had very limited interaction followed by the well-building attempt. In the *Mars* scenario, we had interaction through attacking agents, though the extent (duration and complexity) of these interactions also remained expandable. A challenge for the future is surely to design complex interactions which are interesting to realize and see in action.

5.2 General

A lesson of the early phase was the awareness that normally neglected *engineering* issues (as opposed to *scientific* ones) are of utmost importance. For example, collecting statistical data or providing visualizations turned out to be as important as the choice and the tuning of the scenarios. Without them it was extremely difficult to analyze why a team behaved as it did.

Using automatically generated statistical data, we can easily retrace a whole simulation's progress by looking at the generated charts instead of watching the whole replay. The charts mainly focused on scenario-specific data, like the development of the score or stability of dominated zones. Furthermore, we were finally able to directly and easily compare different simulation runs without having to keep a lot of details in mind. Such tools cannot only be used for debugging the teams' agents, but also for analysis of the scenario and improving it for the next round.

These insights went into the *Agents-on-Mars* scenario, where we noted an increasing number of multi-agent platforms. Since then, our scenarios have always been won by dedicated agent platforms—they seem to outperform "ad-hoc" solutions. This might be attributed to some teams taking part repeatedly, but it also points to an increasing maturity and ease of use concerning multi-agent platforms.

If you followed the years in which each scenario was used closely, you may have noticed that 2015 was missing. That particular year should have been the start of the "City Scenario". We introduced it in 2015, though we might have underestimated its complexity and readiness. As the contest date neared, the participants asked us to postpone the competition, which we did. It moved to early 2016 first and finally to the regular 2016 Contest slot. If we say complexity here, we mean the effort that was required to get a simple agent team running and dealing with all important stages of the game. We learned that, as often requested in the earlier years, we need to publish a completely new scenario as early in the year as possible. We also saw a relative core base of teams that participated in each of the three City contests. While this might tell us that teams who have made the big time investment once are likely to stick around, it is also off-putting for new teams if they have to put in a lot of work to only see some basic results. For the next scenario (Agents Assemble), we always had the concept of *easy to start, hard to master* at the back of our minds.

In order to better understand the underlying strategies of the teams, we worked out a standardized questionnaire [1] (which was further improved over the years). This did not only help to learn about the systems and the results they produced, but also to understand the whole development process. Additionally, it serves for newcomers to avoid mistakes from previous iterations.

The motivation to enter the MAPCwas for some teams simply to learn about multi-agent systems or to refine programming skills. Furthermore, most teams shared our goal of evaluating multi-agent frameworks and platforms. Regarding their structure, teams were composed of students as well as researchers with their background mostly in MAS or at least in artificial intelligence in general. This reinforced our motivation to always come up with new scenarios, rather than optimizing a particular one over the years, which only favors teams that attend each and every year (it seems this happened in the simulation league of the soccer competition).

We also asked the teams how difficult it was and how much effort had to be put into getting to a point where their system behaved as it finally did. We got very diverse results, ranging from only a hundred to over a thousand hours and 1000 to many thousands of lines of code that had to be written, tested and debugged. This clearly hints at varying levels of usability concerning different agent platforms.

Furthermore, teams noted that they not only debugged their agents but found and fixed bugs in the agent framework or platform they used as well, which shows that the MAPCcan play a major role concerning the development and evaluation of different platforms. Nevertheless, the teams are still not satisfied with available state-of-the-art debugging tools, since it requires a lot of effort to debug even 20 agents, each with its own individual mindset.

We realized that the visualization and playability of the respective scenario is a key to reaching a broader audience, especially students, e.g. when *MASSim* is used in teaching in various courses all over the world. The competitive nature is fun for the students and this feature should never be underestimated. To this day, we cannot make out a clear correlation between the specific scenario and the number of participants. A more important factor is usually whether the interested teams are able to invest the necessary time. Similarly, the scenario doesn't seem to have a big impact on the choice of programming language or framework. Most teams either choose a framework they are already familiar with or one they want to learn, but have already heard about (from colleagues or supervisors).

Finally, coming back to our questions raised at the beginning of this paper, namely about the situations where using agent technology pays off and the strengths of agent platforms. For one, we note that the top-performing approaches are usually agent-based. Nonetheless, we have also seen conventional approaches achieve remarkable results. In situations where it is easier to take a global perspective (e.g. the City scenario), conventional approaches or even *centralized* solutions in general, usually seem to have it easier compared to situations where agents have to base their decisions mostly on their local information. Over the years, there has been no clear indication of whether agent-based solutions take less time to create or are smaller in nature. The teams that have used an agent-based approach tend to report their overall satisfaction with their chosen technology though. In the end, it may even be a surprising result that both paradigms almost see eye to eye in our test cases, as the conventional paradigms have been developed over much more time, by vastly more people and see usage that isn't even comparable to agent-oriented programming. If agent programming had a comparable maturity and similarly sophisticated tools, and if people were trained in its use as they are in traditional programming, we might see way shorter development times and in turn even better results.

6   Challenges and Outlook

While the agent paradigm plays an important role in computer science, its uptake in industry still remains small. We believe that the MAPCplays some role in determining under which conditions agent languages can be used in practice.

The ideal scenario we were (and still are) looking for, should be easily testable and not be based on difficult rules (only the solutions should be difficult), so that beginners in the area of agent programming can easily take on the challenge. A good solution should use cooperation among autonomous agents and be flexible enough so that different groups of agents evolve and work together to solve intermediate tasks.

After almost 15 years of research and experience, we still have not found such a *convincing scenario*. Nor have we yet proved that agent-based approaches are clearly superior to other, sometimes even ad-hoc, approaches using traditional programming languages. In many areas of computer science, one is often looking for a *killer application*. However, it may well be that such killer applications do not exist. In defense of MAS, there are many potential advantages that the contest is not evaluating at all, because it does not seem feasible in the context of the competition: reusability, maintenance, correctness, the possibility to model-check agents, code running on different platforms, etc.

Regardless, there are good reasons to be optimistic, because there is progress on two sides. First, multi-agent programming technologies are becoming more and more capable. Secondly, there are many lessons learned throughout the history of the contest and we are getting better at encouraging the cooperative behaviors we want to see in agents.

So what are possible ways to improve our MAPC? We are considering the idea to let *more than two* teams participate in the same simulation. The current scenario would provide for this naturally, however, we need to address better visualization (too many things happening at the same time) and evaluation (to easily find interesting situations and emergent behavior) first.

Our ultimate vision is an agent platform that allows to deploy agents written in very different agent languages, using the specific features of them. For example, it might be beneficial for BDI agents to solve very efficiently certain tasks, whereas planning agents based on some form of *hierarchical task nets* could do the planning for them. Being able to re-use agents already developed (and based on different paradigms) would certainly push the envelope for applications of multi-agent systems in general.

Agents running on a local platform (rather than participating over the Internet) would also allow more fine-grained control over communication and real-time aspects. We could then consider *many* agents, not just a few, but hundreds or thousands of *sophisticated* agents — traditional approaches do not seem to perform well in such a situation. Moreover, with many *interacting agents* we might see some interesting behavior evolve.

However, the price to pay is to standardize the communication and set up common protocols and interfaces for such agents. That would change our contest drastically.

Acknowledgment. The authors would like to thank Alfred Hofmann from Springer for his continuous support right from the beginning, and for endowing the prize of 500 Euros in Springer books.

Also, we extend our gratitude to all anonymous reviewers who helped us make improvements to this paper.

The fourth author acknowledges that his part in this study was financed by the Coordenação de Aperfeiçoamento de Pessoal de Nível Superior – Brasil (CAPES) – Finance Code 001.

Last but not least, we thank all teams that entered our Contest in the last 15 years and helped to keep it alive. The second author sends a special thank you to some former PhD students in his group: Peter Novák, Tristan Behrens, Federico Schlesinger, and Michael Köster. Without their ideas and enthusiasm, the MAPCwould not have flourished.

References

1. Ahlbrecht, T., et al.: Multi-agent programming contest 2013: the teams and the design of their systems. In: Cossentino, M., El Fallah Seghrouchni, A., Winikoff, M. (eds.) EMAS 2013. LNCS (LNAI), vol. 8245, pp. 366–390. Springer, Heidelberg (2013). https://doi.org/10.1007/978-3-642-45343-4_22

2. Ahlbrecht, T., Dix, J., Fiekas, N.: Multi-agent programming contest 2016. Int. J. Agent-Oriented Softw. Eng. **6**(1), 58–85 (2018)

3. Ahlbrecht, T., Dix, J., Fiekas, N.: Multi-agent programming contest 2017 - the twelfth edition of the MAPC. Ann. Math. Artif. Intell. **84**(1), 1–16 (2018). https://doi.org/10.1007/s10472-018-9594-x

4. Ahlbrecht, T., Dix, J., Fiekas, N. (eds.): MAPC 2018. LNCS (LNAI), vol. 11957. Springer, Cham (2019). https://doi.org/10.1007/978-3-030-37959-9

5. Ahlbrecht, T., Dix, J., Köster, M., Schlesinger, F.: Multi-agent programming contest 2013. In: Cossentino, M., El Fallah Seghrouchni, A., Winikoff, M. (eds.) EMAS 2013. LNCS (LNAI), vol. 8245, pp. 292–318. Springer, Heidelberg (2013). https://doi.org/10.1007/978-3-642-45343-4_16

6. Behrens, T., Dastani, M., Dix, J., Köster, M., Novák, P.: The multi-agent programming contest from 2005–2010. Ann. Math. Artif. Intell. **59**(3–4), 277–311 (2010). https://doi.org/10.1007/s10472-010-9219-5

7. Behrens, T.M., Hindriks, K.V., Dix, J.: Towards an environment interface standard for agent platforms. Ann. Math. Artif. Intell. **61**(4), 261–295 (2011). https://doi.org/10.1007/s10472-010-9215-9

8. Boissier, O., Bordini, R.H., Hübner, J.F., Ricci, A., Santi, A.: Multi-agent oriented programming with JaCaMo. Sci. Comput. Program. **78**(6), 747–761 (2013)

9. Bordini, R., Dastani, M., Dix, J., Segrouchni, A.E.F. (eds.): Special Issue on Multi-Agent Programming. J. Auton. Agents Multi-Agent Syst. **23** (2011). http://www.springerlink.com/content/y3621v0p2217h683/. Springer

10. Bordini, R.H., Hübner, J.F., Wooldridge, M.: Programming Multi-agent Systems in AgentSpeak Using Jason, vol. 8. Wiley, Hoboken (2007)

11. Bratman, M., et al.: Intention, Plans, and Practical Reason, vol. 10. Harvard University Press, Cambridge (1987)

12. Genesereth, M., Love, N., Pell, B.: General game playing: overview of the AAAI competition. AI Mag. **26**(2), 62 (2005)

13. Hindriks, K.V.: Programming rational agents in GOAL. In: El Fallah Seghrouchni, A., Dix, J., Dastani, M., Bordini, R.H. (eds.) Multi-Agent Programming, pp. 119–157. Springer, Boston, MA (2009). https://doi.org/10.1007/978-0-387-89299-3_4

14. Johnson, M., Jonker, C., van Riemsdijk, B., Feltovich, P.J., Bradshaw, J.M.: Joint activity testbed: blocks world for teams (BW4T). In: Aldewereld, H., Dignum, V., Picard, G. (eds.) ESAW 2009. LNCS (LNAI), vol. 5881, pp. 254–256. Springer, Heidelberg (2009). https://doi.org/10.1007/978-3-642-10203-5_26
15. Karakovskiy, S., Togelius, J.: The Mario AI benchmark and competitions. IEEE Trans. Comput. Intell. AI Games 4(1), 55–67 (2012)
16. Ketter, W., Collins, J., Reddy, P.: Power TAC: a competitive economic simulation of the smart grid. Energy Econ. 39, 262–270 (2013)
17. Vallati, M., Chrpa, L., Grześ, M., McCluskey, T.L., Roberts, M., Sanner, S., et al.: The 2014 international planning competition: progress and trends. AI Mag. 36(3), 90–98 (2015)
18. Visser, A., Ito, N., Kleiner, A.: RoboCup rescue simulation innovation strategy. In: Bianchi, R.A.C., Akin, H.L., Ramamoorthy, S., Sugiura, K. (eds.) RoboCup 2014. LNCS (LNAI), vol. 8992, pp. 661–672. Springer, Cham (2015). https://doi.org/10.1007/978-3-319-18615-3_54

Contest Entries

LFC: Combining Autonomous Agents and Automated Planning in the Multi-Agent Programming Contest

Rafael C. Cardoso$^{(\boxtimes)}$, Angelo Ferrando , and Fabio Papacchini

University of Liverpool, Liverpool L69 3BX, UK
{rafael.cardoso,angelo.ferrando,fabio.papacchini}@liverpool.ac.uk

Abstract. The 2019 Multi-Agent Programming Contest introduced a new scenario, Agents Assemble, where two teams of agents move around a 2D grid and compete to assemble complex block structures. In this paper, we describe the strategies used by our team that led us to achieve first place in the contest. Our strategies tackle some of the major challenges in the 2019 contest: how to explore and build a map when agents only have access to local vision and no global coordinates; how to move around the map efficiently even though there are dynamic events that can change the cells in the grid; and how to assemble and submit complex block structures given that the opposing team may try to sabotage us. To implement our strategies, we use the multi-agent systems development platform JaCaMo to program our agents and the Fast Downward planner to plan the movement of the agent in the grid. We also provide a brief discussion of our matches in the contest and give our analysis of how our team performed in each match.

Keywords: Multi-Agent Programming Contest · Multi-agent systems · Automated Planning · Agents Assemble · JaCaMo

1 Introduction

The Multi-Agent Programming Contest (MAPC) is an annual event to promote the use and improvement of agent programming languages. A number of teams face off in a challenging scenario that is made to encourage the use of agent techniques. The matches between teams (the clients) are played in a simulated environment (the server) where agents receive perceptions about the environment and can send actions to the server. The simulation occurs synchronously through simulation steps, that is, each agent is required to send its actions to the server before the step deadline (usually four seconds). The team with the highest

Work supported by UK Research and Innovation, and EPSRC Hubs for Robotics and AI in Hazardous Environments: EP/R026092 (FAIR-SPACE), EP/R026173 (ORCA), and EP/R026084 (RAIN).

T. Ahlbrecht et al. (Eds.): MAPC 2019, LNAI 12381, pp. 31–58, 2020.
https://doi.org/10.1007/978-3-030-59299-8_2

score at the end of the match wins the round and is awarded some points. The winner of the contest is the team with the most points.

The 2019 MAPC introduced the Agents Assemble scenario. In this scenario, two teams of ten agents each compete to assemble complex block structures. Blocks can have different types and can be generated upon using the *request* action at a block *dispenser* of the desired type. The environment is represented in a 2D grid where each cell can contain different types of entities and/or terrain: a block; a block dispenser; an obstacle (prohibited cell); an agent; a goal cell; and/or an empty cell. Each agent only has local coordinates of the map (i.e., their position is always 0, 0). Each match has three rounds, and the map used in each round is generated randomly. A complete description of the scenario is available in [1]. For the remainder of this paper, we only describe the features of the scenario that are relevant to the strategy being discussed.

Our team, the Liverpool Formidable Constructors (LFC), achieved first place in the 2019 MAPC. In this paper we discuss the main strategies that our agents used throughout the contest: grid exploration, identification of teammates, evaluation of good goal positions, creating and maintaining a global map, planning an efficient path, and task achievement. A key aspect that differentiates our team from others, even teams from past MAPCs, is the use of a classical planner to plan the movement of our agents in the grid. The LFC source code, as used in the 2019 MAPC, is available at: <https://github.com/autonomy-and-verification-uol/mapc2019-liv>.

This paper is organised as follows. In the next section we describe the software architecture used in the development of our team, namely the Multi-Agent System (MAS) development platform JaCaMo [2] and the Fast Downward planner [6]. Section 3 contains the strategies that we used to solve some of the major challenges present in the Agents Assemble scenario. In Sect. 4 we discuss and analyse our performance in all of our matches in the contest. Section 5 includes a questionnaire created by the contest organisers with short answers about our team. We end the paper with conclusions in Sect. 6.

2   Software Architecture

In this section we describe the two main software tools that we used to develop our solution to the 2019 MAPC. First, we describe the MAS development platform JaCaMo [2] and the features that we made use of to develop our agents and interact with the environment. Then, we discuss the Fast Downward planner [6] and how we integrated it into our JaCaMo agents so that they could call their own planner to plan an optimal path.

2.1   JaCaMo

The JaCaMo[1] [2] development platform allows Multi-Agent System (MAS) to be programmed at several abstraction layers: organisation, agent, and environment. At the top layer the organisation is defined using Moise [8] where groups,

---

[1] http://jacamo.sourceforge.net/.

roles, links, plan coordination, and norms can be specified. These concepts can be utilised in the middle layer by the Jason [3] agents that are programmed following the Belief Desire Intention (BDI) model [11]. The BDI model consists of three mental attitudes: *beliefs* represent the agent's knowledge about the world (including itself), *desires* are goal states that the agent wants to bring about, and *intentions* are partial descriptions of actions to achieve some state. The third layer is defined by CArtAgO [12] artifacts. These artifacts are used to describe the environment. An artifact can have *observable properties* that represent the perceptions coming from the environment, and *operations* that describe the outcome of actions in the environment.

Most of the fundamental code architecture in JaCaMo, such as the interface between our agents and the server, has been imported from past participation in the contest from one of our team members, specifically the team PUCRS in 2016 [5], team SMART-JaCaMo in 2017 [4], and team SMART_JaCaMo in 2018 [9]. We used a snapshot of version 0.7 of JaCaMo. The specific library is available in the `lib` folder of the repository containing our code.

In terms of the Jason agents we mostly developed from scratch, but still retained some of the architecture from previous years. We kept the use of modules, first used and described in [4], to better keep track of beliefs pertaining to each strategy and to help in the debug of the system. We also used the reasoning engine to reconsider agent's intentions, first introduced in [9]. This is useful for agents to be able to change the action that they want to perform before sending it to server. Actions are only sent to the server once all agents in our team have selected an action to perform. It may be the case that an agent selects an action, but then receives information from another agent that causes it to reconsider its own action. We made some small changes to this engine to fit our needs in the new scenario.

In CArtAgO, we use the same structure from previous years. A `Translator` class is used to translate information from agents to the server (literal to action and terms to parameters) and from the server to the agents (perception to literal and parameters to terms). There is one environment artifact (`EISArtifact`) per agent that acts as the agent interface with the server. This artifact also contains the interface with the planner (discussed in the next section). The interface with the server is responsible for registering the agents to the server, collecting and filtering perceptions from the server, and transmitting the actions chosen by the agents. For more details on the functionality of these features we refer the reader to previous papers [4,5,9].

Apart from the planner interface and updated perception filter (to match the beliefs of the new scenario), the only new addition to the environment artifact is the position of the agent, which is initialised with the (0, 0) coordinates. We opted to keep this information in the agent's artifact instead of the agent's belief base because it was easier to keep it consistent after map merges.

Lastly, we have the usual `TeamArtifact` that is used to share information among all agents in the team. This artifact is very useful to maintain shared data free of race conditions without spending time implementing semaphores and locks to each data structure that agents want to share with the whole team. The `TeamArtifact` was even more useful than in previous years due to the necessity of sharing (and merging) the maps and the dynamic environment of the new scenario. We discuss the particular operations and observable properties of this artifact in the relevant strategy section (see Sect. 3 for the descriptions of our strategies).

We have an ad-hoc implementation of roles using the `my_role` belief to keep track of which role the agent is playing and some plans that the agents can use to update this belief. Unfortunately, we did not implement these roles in Moise, due to lack of time we had to prioritise other features. Thus, we were not able to use any of the organisation related features that Moise offers in JaCaMo, such as role hierarchy, groups, automatic plans for adopting/abandoning roles/groups, automatic tracking of beliefs related to roles and the organisation, plan coordination, among others. We hope to make use of Moise in the next iterations of the scenario.

2.2   Fast Downward

To improve our agents' movement, we used version 19.06 of the Fast Downward (FD) planning system[2] ([6] and [7]). A detailed explanation on how we used FD to improve our agents' movements is given in Sect. 3.6, but the high-level idea is that we wanted to use an off-the-shelf planner able to produce optimal answers within the 4 s time limit that agents are required to send their action. We selected FD for several reasons. First, it is a well-established planner which has participated several times in the International Planning Competition (IPC). Second, its results at the IPC in 2018[3] were promising as the planner performed well in two of the classical tracks, the satisficing track and the bounded-cost track[4]. Finally, one of our team members already had some experience with the planner.

The main drawback in using FD as the chosen planner was the lack of support for numerical planning. Specifically, while it is possible in the planning language to express statement such as "a clear action requires at least 30 energy to be performed", the FD planner would ignore such information. However, because FD supports action costs, we were able to devise a workaround the numerical limitation by defining the clear action as the most expensive action (i.e., it requires 3 steps to be performed) and then search for plans with minimal action cost. This workaround can still result in unfeasible plans, but we refer to Sect. 3.6 for more details.

Due to testing with the planner and the need for fast prototyping, integration with JaCaMo was rather rudimentary. Specifically, we implemented a simple shell script to become familiar with and to test the planner. The script invokes the planner with the following command line arguments:

---

[2] http://www.fast-downward.org/.

[3] https://ipc2018.bitbucket.io/.

[4] https://ipc2018-classical.bitbucket.io/#results.

- --sas-file agent_name.sas: the planner creates a sas file named "agent_name" (i.e., each agent has its own file) which contains a translation of the planning problem used as input for the planner;
- --plan-file agent_name_output: if a plan is returned by the planner, then it is written into a file named "agent_name_output";
- --search-time-limit 1 s: it limits the search time to one second, this was necessary in order to stay under the 4 s time limit;
- --alias seq-opt-lmcut: selection of a predefined search strategy for optimisation problems that had the best results in our tests; and
- the last two parameters were the domain and problem files written in PDDL (Planning Domain Definition Language) [10].

If a plan is returned within the one second time limit, then the script parses the output file, reprints the plan in a suitable format, and removes existing sas and output files.

On the JaCaMo side, once an agent decides to use the planner it checks in the TeamArtifact whether it is allowed to invoke the planner. This operation performs a simple check of how many agents are currently calling a planner. This was needed when testing our code in slower computers, but during the contest the maximum value of concurrent agents calling a planner was set to 10 (the maximum number of agents in a team), since the computer we were using could comfortably handle 10 simultaneous planner instances. In case of positive answer, it sends its intended goal position to the EISArtifact. The EISArtifact creates an opportune problem file based on (1) what is in the agent's vision, and (2) what is the agent's goal. The domain file was created at design time, since it is static and does not change. The script is called as soon as the problem file is created, and then the script output is parsed. If no plan is found, then the scripts simply prints "NO PLAN". If either "NO PLAN" is returned, or an error occurred during the process, then an empty plan is returned to the agent. Details on how agents manage different planner outcomes are described in Sect. 3.6.

3 Strategies and Behaviours

Strategies are what define the main behaviour of our agents. A strategy contains the details on how to solve a particular problem, such as exploring the map or achieving a task. The strategy that each agent uses is based on the beliefs and goals that it has. This is done individually by each agent at key steps in the simulation (i.e., when trigger events of certain strategies occur) and an agent may play multiple strategies in the same step. For example, when an agent is exploring the map and finds another agent of its team both agents momentarily swap to the agent identification strategy. Then, after the identification is complete they revert back to their previous strategy.

3.1 Exploration

The map used in a round is a randomly generated grid of unknown dimensions. Agents are able to see up to five blocks away, as shown in Fig. 1. Any perception received about cells in an agent's vision are oriented using the agent's local coordinates, which is always position (0, 0). In other words, at any step in a simulation each agent's local position is (0, 0). This remains true even after the agent moves. Therefore, at the start of the simulation it is important to explore the surroundings to try to find goal positions and dispensers of different block types.

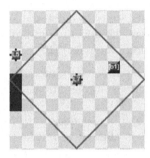

Fig. 1. The diamond area represents the vision of agent L7. In this example, L7 perceives that there is an obstacle at (−5, 0) and a dispenser for blocks of type b1 at (3, −1). It does not perceive anything else outside this area (e.g., it cannot see agent L5).

There is no use in sharing information about what agents see unless they have access to a global map. However, to be able to create such a map and share information, first these agents have to see each other at least once. Although we have strategies for creating this map (discussed in following sections), for exploration we ignore the global map entirely and each agent only uses its vision to decide what direction to explore (north, south, east or west). Note that using information from the global map (or even the agent's local map) to inform exploration may be more advantageous, but in our tests our current approach proved to be sufficient in exploring most of the map. There is a trade-off between the time necessary for implementing the code for such a complex strategy and a *mostly* random approach to exploration. Although we considered this trade-off not to be worth it, in future contests this should be re-evaluated.

Our agents select a random direction from the list of possible directions, initially containing all four: north, south, east, and west (as exemplified in Fig. 2a). For any subsequent step, the agent will follow the same direction as long as it remains valid. A direction is no longer valid if there is an obstruction at distance less than or equal to 2. For the purposes of this check, we consider an obstruction to be either an obstacle or a block. An example of this is shown in Fig. 2b, where there are two obstacles at (1, 0) and (−1, 0) of the agent (removing east and of the list of valid directions), and a block at (0, −2) of the agent (removing north). Therefore, the only remaining valid direction is south.

When the chosen direction is no longer valid, both the direction and the opposite direction are removed from the list of valid directions. For example, if the agent was moving south and encounters an obstruction, both south and north are removed from the list.

If the list of valid directions is empty, then we relax our obstruction condition and call a special case with two stages. In both stages, the obstruction condition is reduced to a distance equal to 1. In the first stage (Fig. 2c), the agent picks a new direction from the list of valid directions (now repopulated with the relaxed obstruction condition, but still without the opposite direction of the last movement). The agent then moves in the chosen direction until there is an obstruction in the next cell. In the second stage (Fig. 2d), the agents picks a second direction, where the list of valid directions contains only the opposite axis of the last movement (e.g. if the agent was moving south, possible directions include east and west, assuming they pass the obstruction condition), and again moves in the chosen direction until there is an obstruction in the next cell. After the special case is completed or if it fails, then the agent reverts back to the normal exploration behaviour.

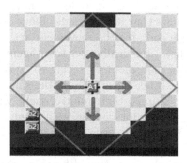

(a) Random direction from [north,south,east,west].

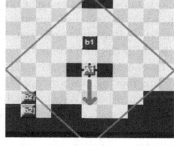

(b) Random direction from [south].

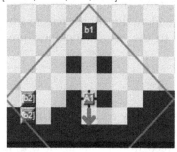

(c) First stage of special exploration.

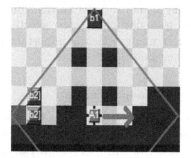

(d) Second stage of special exploration.

Fig. 2. Different behaviours in exploration.

During the normal exploration behaviour (i.e., not in the special case), if agents encounter an obstruction in the direction that they are moving, they will try to execute the *clear* action to remove it as long as they are above a certain *energy threshold*. We used 240 as the threshold, out of a maximum energy of 300. During the contest, a successful clear action had a cost of 30 energy, thus, our agents were able to perform up to two clears while exploring, but still save a reasonable amount of energy for future clears to be used in more important strategies. Longer exploration phases would allow for more clear actions, since agents gained 1 energy per round, up to the maximum amount of energy.

Even though we are using a simple strategy for exploration, there are some conditionals that can be taken into consideration to improve the overall behaviour of the agents that are exploring. For example, it is possible (although somewhat unlikely) that there are teammates in each of the adjacent four directions. In such a case, the agent should attempt to move by selecting one direction randomly out of all four directions.

It is possible (although rare) that the agent will end up with no valid direction to choose from (e.g., an empty direction list) and with an obstruction in all four directions. In such case, the agent will skip a step and then try to clear blocks before reassessing the direction list. Other corner cases include dealing with an out of bounds movement (the agent only knows that it is trying to move outside of the grid when it receives a specific failure code for the movement action) by simply removing that direction from the list, and dealing with an agent from the same team in the immediate direction of movement by trying to go around the agent by choosing the relative right (the other agent will do the same, and since they are moving towards opposite directions, their relative right will be different to each other). We did not have a plan for dealing with agents from the other team. In such case, our agents would simply keep trying to move until being successful.

We considered other viable options for exploration that differ from random direction or movement based on map information, such as picking a single direction for all agents to move or distributing 1/4 of the directions to each agent. However, from our initial tests, selecting a random direction seems to work best across most maps, which is important due to the map randomness present in each simulation.

3.2 Agent Identification

In order to cooperate the agents have to first identify each other. Unfortunately, when the game starts the agents do not have this information. When an agent meets another one in its vision it can only recognise if that agent is a member of its own team. Because of this, one of the first challenges we had to tackle was agent identification. That is, when an agent meets another one of its team, it has to try to identify exactly which agent it is.

Each step, when an agent receives the perceptions from the server, they are checked if there is an unknown entity in its vision which is part of its team. When this happens, a broadcast message is triggered and the agent (let us call it A_0) asks to all the agents in its team (let us call them $A_1, \ldots, A_n$) to communicate what they are currently seeing in their vision at this time step. Each agent receiving this broadcast message replies with a list containing all the thing perceptions it has.

When A_0 receives all the replies, the identification process begins. For each reply, A_0 analyses the list of things that were reported. First, it has to understand if the reply is from an agent in its vision. For each replying agent A_i, A_0 checks if in the list of things there is one entity with relative position (X, Y) and in its beliefs there is an entity with relative position (-X, -Y). If this is true, then it means that it is possible that A_i and A_0 are currently seeing each other, since both see an entity of their team in the symmetric position. However, this is not enough because there can be multiple agents on the map which are at the same distance and relative position. In order to differentiate these cases, the identification process requires a second step, where for all the things contained in the list, A_0 has to check if these are also in its perceptions. Naturally, this is limited to only the things which are in A_0's vision. If after this step only one agent A_i satisfies these constraints, then A_0 knows that the agent in its vision is A_i. If instead, after this step more than one agent is still suitable for being the agent in vision, then A_0 cannot conclude the identity of the entity, and the identification process ends. In the following time steps, until A_0 has not identified all the agents in its team, it will keep trying to identify each unknown agent.

In Algorithm 1 we report the pseudo-code for the identification process. The algorithm is triggered when an unknown entity enters the vision of the agent. To simplify the presentation, we assume unification in the conditions, and where we are not interested in the value of a parameter we use the _ symbol.

Algorithm 1: identify()

```
1   Trigger: an unknown entity entered my vision;
2   if I see an unknown teammate in position (X, Y) then
3       broadcast a request for info to all teammates;
4       set candidates = [ ];
5       for each teammate A_i do
6           wait reply containing list L of things seen by A_i;
7           if thing(-X, -Y, entity, myTeam) in L then
8               possible = true;
9               for each thing(W, Z, Type, Name) in L do
10                  if |X+W| + |Y+Z| ≤ 5 and thing(X+W, Y+Z, _, _) not in my
                       beliefs then
11                      possible = false;
12                      break;
13              if possible then
14                  add A_i to candidates;
15       if length(candidates) == 1 then
16           add A_i to the list of identified agents
```

In order to better understand how the identification process works, we report a simple example. In this scenario, shown in Fig. 3, we have two agents of the same team involved, A5 and A3.

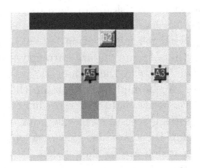

Fig. 3. Identification example with two agents and a dispenser.

For simplicity we focus on the identification process on A5's side (for A3 is symmetric). In this example, we suppose A5 has not identified A3 yet, and when the belief thing(4, 0, entity, ''A'') is added in its belief base, it broadcasts a request for information to all the agents in its team. When A3 receives this request, it sends to A5 the list of things is currently seeing in its vision: [thing(-4, 0, entity, ''A''), thing(-3, -2, dispenser, b2)]. With this information, A5 first has to check if there is an entity in the list in position (X, Y), and a corresponding entity in its belief base in position (-X, -Y). This is satisfied, in fact thing(-4, 0, entity, ''A'') is in the list returned by A3, and in the A5's belief base, we have thing(4, 0, entity, ''A''). Thus, it is possible that the agent in A5's vision is A3. But, to be sure of it, A5 also has to check that all the things thing(W, Z, Type, Name), in the list which are in its vision ($|W+X| + |Z+Y| \leq 5$) are also present in its belief base; meaning that we can find thing(W+X, Z+Y, Type, Name) in the belief base for each thing in the list (where X and Y are the relative coordinates of A3 from A5's viewpoint).

In this very simple example X = 4, Y = 0 and the list contains only thing(-3, -2, dispenser, b2). Since $|-3+4| + |-2+0| = |1| + |-2| = 3 \leq 5$, the dispenser should also be in A5's vision, and it is, in fact we have thing(1, -2, dispenser, b2) in A5's belief base. Supposing that there are not other teammates at the same distance, A5 can safely conclude that the agent in its vision is A3. The same thing is be done by A3, which will identify A5 as the agent in its own vision.

3.3 Goal Evaluation

In this section, we present how an agent evaluates a goal position. We need this additional step because we want to pick a suitable goal position to be used when solving the tasks later on. The task completion (see Sect. 3.7) is expensive in terms of preparation and communication among the agents; thus, the agents have to ensure that they pick a good goal position. More specifically, a goal position is considered suitable when it has enough space around it for the agents to assemble block structures and to complete the tasks.

Algorithm 2: move_to(X2, Y2)

Data: Target position (X2,Y2)

1 **get** agent position (X1,Y1);
2 **while** *not (X1,Y1) == (X2,Y2)* **do**
3   direction = w;
4   distance = |X1-1-X2| + |Y1-Y2|;
5   **if** $|X1{+}1{-}X2| + |Y1{-}Y2| \leq distance$ **then**
6   direction = e;
7   distance = |X1+1-X2| + |Y1-Y2|;
8   **if** $|X1{-}X2| + |Y1{-}1{-}Y2| \leq distance$ **then**
9   direction = n;
10   distance = |X1-X2| + |Y1-1-Y2|;
11 **if** $|X1{-}X2| + |Y1{+}1{-}Y2| \leq distance$ **then**
12   direction = s;
13   distance = |X1-X2| + |Y1+1-Y2|;
14 **if** *direction is blocked by obstacle* **then**
15   **if** *distance $\leq$ 3* **or** *(**not** go_around(direction) **and** enough energy)* **then**
16   clear in direction of the target;
17   **else**
18   skip;
19 **else**
20   move(direction);
21 **get** agent position (X1,Y1);

In the goal evaluation process, since the movement required by the agents is not complex, the agents do not call the planner to plan for an optimal path. Calling the planner is computationally expensive, thus it is best to be avoided when possible. For this specific task, we developed a simplified movement algorithm which allows the agents to move and evaluate the goal position. This algorithm is composed of two parts: direction selection and obstacle avoidance. Assuming the agent has to move to a specific position; in order to choose in which direction the agent should move, it computes the Manhattan distance between its current position and the target destination. Then, the agent moves to the neighbouring cell which minimises the distance that was evaluated. A high-level description of the move_to function is reported in Algorithm 2. The advantage of this approach lies in being fast, in fact it is not required to compute the entire path in advance, but at each step the agent simply picks the cell which brings it closer to the final destination. Even though this makes the approach very efficient, the presence of obstacles on the path can be a problem. For instance, the closest cell to the final destination can be occupied by an obstacle.

Algorithm 3: go_around(D)

Data: D is the direction to the obstacle

1   **if** $D == n$ **or** $D == s$ **then**
2   OpposideD = opposite direction of D;
3   **if** *there is a gap in direction w* **then**
4   Ds = [(w,D),(D,e),(e,OpposideD),(OpposideD,w)];
5   **else if** *there is a gap in direction e* **then**
6   Ds = [(e,D),(D,w),(w,OpposideD),(OpposideD,e)];
7   **else**
8   **return** *false*;

9   **else**
10   OpposideD = opposite direction of D;
11   **if** *there is a gap in direction n* **then**
12   Ds = [(n,D),(D,s),(s,OpposideD),(OpposideD,n)];
13   **else if** *there is a gap in direction s* **then**
14   Ds = [(s,D),(D,n),(n,OpposideD),(OpposideD,s)];
15   **else**
16   **return** *false*;

17 **while** *Ds* **is not** *empty* **do**
18   **get** and **remove** first tuple (DtoGo,DTarget) from Ds;
19   **while** *cell in direction DTarget contains obstacle* **and** *new direction to target is not the opposite of DTarget* **do**
20   **if** *cell in direction DtoGo does not contain obstacle* **then**
21   move(DtoGo);
22   **else**
23   **return** *false*

24 **return** *true*;

We implemented an obstacle avoidance algorithm which allows the agent to go around the obstacles on its path. The high-level description of this is reported in Algorithm 3. In this algorithm, the agent knows there is an obstacle in a specific direction D, and it wants to go around it. Depending on D, the agent creates a projection of the path to avoid the obstacle. Since an obstacle can have two alternative directions to be passed, the agent picks the direction considering the presence of gaps in the path. If the agent sees a gap which could be used to pass the obstacle, it favours that direction over the other. The path projection is coded as a list, which is then used by the agent to move around the obstacle. For brevity and clarity of the presentation, we omit technical details such as:

considering action failures and the possibility of having obstacles composed by infinite blocks (although in the contest this never happened).

Now that we have presented the movement used by the agent during goal evaluation, we describe how the actual process of evaluating a goal works. We need to evaluate a goal position due to the complexity of the task completion process. In this evaluation, we check that all the requirements we need to complete the tasks later on are satisfied by the chosen goal position.

The goal evaluation process starts when an agent discovers in its vision a new goal position. First, it has to understand if this goal position belongs to a cluster (set of goals) which has been already evaluated. In order to do that, the agents sharing the same map maintain a list of discovered clusters. A new goal position is added to the closest cluster, i.e., the cluster whose goals are closest to the new one. If no cluster is close enough, it means the new goal belongs to a new cluster and consequently a new cluster containing this single goal position is added to the list. When this happens, it means the agent has discovered a new cluster, which has to be evaluated. The agent that discovered it stops exploring the map and starts evaluating the new cluster.

First, the agent moves to the goal position discovered. Then, it finds the center of the cluster; depending on the form of the cluster there could be multiple centers, in which case one is randomly picked. Once the center is selected, the agent moves to the center. From that position, the agent tries to clear in the 4 cardinal directions, at distance 5 (the maximum in its range). If all the clear attempts succeed, then the goal cluster is suitable since there is enough space around for the task completion (e.g., the positions cleared are not outside the grid of the map). After that, the agent has to find the positions around the cluster which will be used by the retriever agents (the agents fetching the blocks and delivering them to the origin agent later on, see Sect. 3.7). These positions are generated on a rectangle around the goal cluster, and the agent goes in each one of them in order to make sure that they are reachable positions. When the agent finds enough positions for the number of retrievers, in this case 9 (10 agents = 1 origin + 9 retrievers), it stops evaluating the cluster and saves the results.

Even though the map can change because of clear events and actions from other agents, thanks to this evaluation process, we have a higher probability that a cluster has enough space around it to allow for the completion of complex tasks. The list of retriever positions around the cluster also guarantees that our retrievers will have enough space to move without risking being stuck or trying to move outside the map.

3.4 Building a Map

Information about the grid, such as dispenser, goal, and block positions are only received when inside the vision of the agent. Thus, our agents have to save this information in order to keep track of the things that it has discovered. In what follows we describe how agents build their local map, and ultimately a global map that consists of the merging of maps from agents that meet each other while they are moving through the grid.

Local Map. Agents can change their position each simulation step; blocks can be moved when attached to an agent or cleared after a clear action/event or after a pattern of blocks is successfully submitted for a task; and obstacles can be cleared. Thus, due to the dynamic environment of the scenario, we only keep the positions of dispensers and goals in the map. Each agents starts with its own local map, with the origin position of the map set to $(0, 0)$. Although this local map is saved to the `TeamArtifact`, initially each agent can only access its own map. There is no reason to access maps from other agents because their coordinates would not match, rendering the information within useless. Overtime, after an agent meets another one for the first time, they will attempt to merge their maps, eventually obtaining a single global map once enough agents have met each other.

Agents also keep track of their global position in their map. This is with respect to the initial origin of the map $(0, 0)$. That is, after each step where a successful movement action was performed by an agent, it updates its global position in that map accordingly. For example, at step 0 A_1 performs move south; at step 0, A_1 perceives that its last action was successful; then, it updates its global position from $(0, 0)$ to $(0, 1)$.

Merging Maps. Two maps are merged when an agent from each map meet. Each agent starts with its own map, we refer to these agents as the leaders of their respective maps. The coordination of the merge happens between the two map leaders. The map that will be merged into another one is decided based on a heuristic: from a list of all the agents, the leader that will coordinate the merge (i.e., the map that will remain) is the leader that appears first in the list (out of these two leaders). For example, consider that we have two agents meet each other A_1 and A_2, from different maps (respectively M_1 and M_2). The map M_1 has agents $[A_1, A_5]$ and M_2 has agents $[A_2, A_3, A_4]$, where the head of the list is the leader of the map (respectively A_1 and A_2). First, we identify the leader with priority: from a list of agents $[A_5, A_3, A_2, A_1, A_4]$ we know that A_2 happens first in the list over A_1. This means that M_1 will be merged into M_2, i.e., the information in M_1 will be added to M_2 and M_1 will be discarded. After the merge, all agents from M_1 are now added to the map M_2.

We show our merge protocol in Fig. 4. It is possible that the leader of map $M1$ is $A1$, in which case the agent sends a message to itself (same result as triggering the intended plan). Similarly, the same applies if the leader of $M2$ is $A2$. It is possible that a merge fails for two reasons: (a) the leader of $M1$ does not have priority over the leader of $M2$ (in which case the merge may be successful when $A2$ tries the merge, instead of $A1$); (b) the leader of $M1$ receives a `merge_cancelled` reply instead of a `merge_confirmed`, which can be caused by a concurrent merge process which blocked the leader of $M2$, and after this concurrent merge was concluded the leader of $M2$ changed. If a merge fails, agents will proceed to the next simulation step, upon which they may try to merge again (if the merge is still valid).

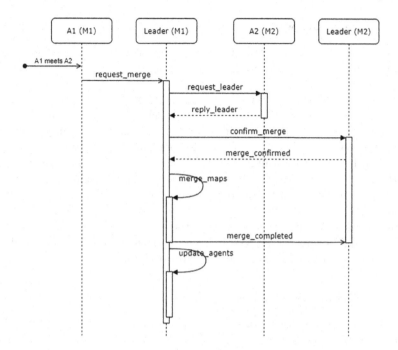

Fig. 4. Sequence diagram for the merge protocol. Usual notation from UML sequence diagram applies: solid arrow heads represent synchronous messages, open arrow heads asynchronous messages, dashed lines represent reply messages, and rectangles represent processes.

There are two important stages in the merging of maps, these are shown in Fig. 4 as the `merge_maps` and `update_agents` calls. The `merge_maps` works as follows:

1. **Calculate new coordinates:** Each dispenser and goal from $M2$ needs to be added to $M1$. However, their coordinates must be updated to consider the origin point of $M1$ instead of $M2$, otherwise their position will not match their real position in the grid. To correctly update these coordinates, we simply have to add to their original X and Y values what we call the new origin coordinates $NewX$ and $NewY$ respectively. We calculate these values as follows: $NewX = (GlobalA1X + LocalA2A1X) - GlobalA2X$, wherein $GlobalA1X$ is the global position of $A1$ in the X axis of $M1$, $LocalA2A1X$ is the position of $A2$ in the X axis according to the local view of $A1$, and $GlobalA2X$ is the global position of $A2$ in the X axis of $M2$. The same is calculated for the $NewY$ value using the Y axis.
2. **Update artifact:** Each new position that was calculated is added in the `TeamArtifact` map structure for $M1$.

The `update_agents` works as follows:

1. **Build new list of identified agents:** the new list of identified agents includes all agents that are a part of $M1$ and $M2$. This will be the new list of members of $M1$.
2. **Send update to the leader of $M2$:** the new list of identified agents and the new origin coordinates $(NewX, NewY)$ are sent to the leader of $M2$, which uses it to update its global position in the new map. This message is sent separately to the leader of $M2$ purely for bookkeeping purposes.
3. **Send update to all agents of $M1$:** the new list of identified agents is sent to the members of $M1$ from before the merge. These agents are staying in their original map, and therefore, they do not need to update their global positions.
4. **Send update to all agents of $M2$:** the new list of identified agents and the new origin coordinates $(NewX, NewY)$ are sent to each member of $M2$, which are used to update their global position in the new map.

3.5   From Exploration to Tasks

Naturally, our agents cannot explore the map forever, and eventually they have to start focusing on completing tasks. The decision of stopping exploration and swapping to task completion can be triggered by two different events: the addition of a new task, or, the merging of two maps. In the first case, the agent has to check it the following conditions are satisfied:

– At least one goal cluster has been found and evaluated positively.
– The agent has identified at least 2 teammates.
– For each block required to complete any one task, the agent knows a dispenser to generate that type of block.

If all the previous conditions are satisfied, it means the agent has gathered enough information from its exploration, and it can start solving tasks.

It is possible that upon the time an agent decides to stop, not all the agents are in the same group (i.e., not all have been identified by the agent which stops). Nonetheless, waiting to have all the agents in the group would be too strict, and would make the approach too slow. Because of this, the group with the agent which has stopped does not wait for the other agents to join it. This brings us to the second event which can make an agent stop exploring, namely when it joins a group which has already stopped. Agents of other groups will keep exploring and eventually will meet an agent of the group that has stopped, and when this happens, they will stop exploring and start retrieving blocks for achieving the tasks.

The first agent which stops exploring becomes the origin for the task resolution. Since the addition of a task is perceived by all the agents, it is possible that multiple agents decide to stop at the same time, but only one will be elected to be origin, while the others will become retrievers. The retrievers and the task origin are discussed further in Sect. 3.7.

3.6   Optimal In-Vision Planning

The movement of agents in a dynamic and unknown map is difficult due to the many edge cases that can be found while attempting to move to a destination. For example: there could be an obstacle/block/agent in the cell the agent is trying to move; there could be a clear event about to happen, which may either disable the agent, remove an obstacle, or spawn an obstacle; etc. In our experience, most of the tricky cases happened when agents had to come together to assemble a block structure. This concentration of agents and blocks makes movement prone to failure if their movement is not precise. For this reason, we use an automated planner for planning the actions (clear, rotate, and movement) of an agent when moving to a target destination (after the exploration phase).

This section describes how agents move in the map once the exploration phase is over. The difference in behaviour between moving during exploration and moving afterwards is due to different focus on the agents' side. Specifically, exploration agents are only concerned in gathering enough information to start performing their tasks, but after the exploration each agent has a specific objective (e.g., retrieving a particular block, or going to a goal position). This implies that after the exploration phase agents have clear destinations to reach. As the map changes constantly due to factors such as clear events or enemy agents moving blocks, we decided to avoid an approach based on what the agents believe the map to look like, and to pursue an approach based on the local vision of agents.

In what follows we present in detail the scenario where an agent wants to reach a specific destination (e.g., next to a dispenser or next to a goal position). The scenario is divided into three parts: selection of a destination; invocation of the FD planner; and managing planner result.

Selection of a Destination. Based on the agent's task, the agent decides to reach a specific destination (given in global coordinates). The agent translates the global coordinates into coordinates relative to its current position. Most likely, the resulting coordinates are not within the agent's vision, and to reach such a destination the agent recursively plans a path to temporary destinations, bringing it closer to the final destination. The selection of temporary destinations is based on heuristics, which try to select 'good cells'. In what follows we refer to a cell as a *good cell* if there is neither an agent nor a block at the time of evaluation. The heuristic used to select a temporary destination is as follows. First, the agent computes the relative coordinates (x, y) of a cell at the border of its vision (i.e., $|x|+|y| = 5$), which represents the cell closest to the destination. If the computed cell is a good cell, then the agent selects such cell as its temporary destination. Otherwise, the agent tries to move either north (resp., south) or east (resp., west) based on whether $|x| < |y|$ and $y < 0$ (resp., $y > 0$), or $|x| > |y|$ and $x > 0$ (resp., $x < 0$). In case it decides to move north (resp., south), it evaluates the cell $(0, -5)$ (resp., $(0, 5)$). The behaviour for moving east (resp., west) is analogous. If the cell is a good cell, then it becomes the temporary destination. Otherwise, the process is repeated for the three closest cells. If no good cell is found during this process, then the agent behaves in the same way as when it receives an empty plan, which is described later on in this section.

Invocation of the FD Planner. In the eventuality that a destination has been selected by the agent, then it invokes the planner in order to plan its next few actions. When invoking the planner, several details need to be provided by the invoking agent. First, the agent has to specify whether or not a block is attached, and what its relative coordinates are. Second, the agent has to specify what is its goal (e.g., the agent wants to reach the destination, or the attached block has to reach the destination). Finally, whether or not the planner is allowed to return a plan using the clear action. The latter information is due to the FD planner not handling numerical planning, but handling action cost optimisation. As mentioned in Sect. 2.2, the heuristic we used is based on the idea that the clear action is the most expensive action since it is the only one requiring three steps. Hence, we regarded unlikely for the planner to return an optimal solution containing more than one clear action. For this reason the agent only checks whether or not it has enough energy to perform at least one clear action. In case of a positive answer the planner is invoked with the possibility of using clear actions, and otherwise such a possibility is forbidden[5]. All the aforementioned information is passed to the `EISArtifact`. The `EISArtifact` already contains information on what is in the agent's vision, and uses such information and the details provided by the agent in order to create a new PDDL problem file. Since we did not want to perform any clear action on blocks attached to allied agents, the domain files do not allow the planner to perform clear actions over blocks. We also did not want to perform clear actions on agents, and decided to treat them as blocks. As soon as the `EISArtifact` has created the PDDL problem file, then it invokes the shell script with the call to the planner and parses its output. If an error occurred during the process of problem creation, or if the planner did not return a solution (i.e., no solution exists or no plan was found within the one second timeout), then an empty plan is returned to the agent. Otherwise, a sequence of actions is returned.

Managing Planner Result. Any returned solution (empty or not) is processed by the agent. If a sequence of actions is returned, then the agent executes them in a rather blind fashion. It can, of course, happen that some action fails (e.g., a random fail occurs, or an unexpected obstacle appears). If the failing action is not a movement action, then the event is simply ignored. Otherwise, the agent tracks the failed movement in order to have an up-to-date information regarding its distance to the destination. There are two reasons for such a forgiving approach to action failures. First, re-invoking the planner can easily result in a huge consumption of resources because the returned plan is based on a snapshot of the agent's vision, and the dynamic nature of the environment will easily lead to

---

[5] From a modelling point of view, allowing or not a clear action is based simply on using a PDDL domain file with or without the definition of the action.

new faulty plans. Second, the agent is getting closer to its destination as long as not all planned actions fail. The situation is different when the returned solution is empty (or if the destination selection heuristic does not find a good cell) since the agent cannot delegate its decision making process to the planner, but it is still required to take a decision. In this case the agent tries to perform a single step movement action before invoking the planner again. The direction of the movement is again based on heuristics involving some of the same ideas as those used for destination selection. The reasoning behind performing one movement action before a new planner invocation is the low likelihood of the situation to stay exactly the same. In other words, we thought that a single action together with the dynamic nature of the environment was enough of a change, which should result in increasing the likelihood for a new planner call to be successful. The heuristics we used resulted in a good performance of our system in this year competition, but they are clearly not optimal yet. In fact, there is at least one example where our heuristics resulted in a loop in an agent's behaviour. Specifically, the loop described in Sect. 4 in round two against the team GOAL-DTU is the result of the environment not changing enough after one time step.

3.7 Achieving Tasks

We only consider tasks in the time step that they have been announced by the server. From experience in past contests, in particular [4,9], we know that it is more advantageous to first build a stock of items that we may require to complete tasks. Then, once we have everything we need to complete the task, we commit to trying to achieve it. A team that uses this strategy of stocking items will always complete a task before a team that first decides on a task and then tries to obtain the necessary items. Since teams share the same pool of tasks, failing a task because the other team completed it first can be very detrimental to the score of the team, since it is very hard to reuse the resources of the failed task to a new task.

Agents that decide to stop exploring will switch their strategy to pursue and achieve tasks. The first agent in the group that decides to stop becomes the *task origin*. The task origin is responsible for:

1. choose a good cluster goal;
2. move to the appropriate goal position within the cluster;
3. clear any blocks or obstacles while idle (i.e., not trying to achieve a particular task);
4. evaluate and select a new task to be achieved;
5. coordinate with the other agents to build the pattern required by the task;
6. submit the task.

The remaining agents from the group will become the retrievers. Retrievers are responsible for building a stock of blocks that can later be used to build block patterns. Retrievers will pick a block from a pool of block types, which is constantly updated to ensure that we have a good variety of blocks available in our stock. After collecting a block, the retriever will move to a designated position (previously scouted during goal evaluation) where it waits for a block request from the task origin.

A task will be selected only if it has been announced in the active step and if there are enough retrievers in position with all of the blocks that the task requires. The task origin contacts the appropriate retrievers to request them to bring their blocks. While some retrievers may bring their blocks in parallel, this is only allowed when it is not possible to have a conflict. In other words, multiple retrievers can bring their blocks in parallel only if the designated position in the pattern does not require a block that another retriever is currently bringing. This constraint is only necessary to alleviate some of the burden from coordinating the agents, and could be removed if proper coordination was in place. Once a retriever adds his block to the pattern, it reverts to its normal behaviour and goes to fetch another block for the stock. After the pattern is complete, the task origin submits the task.

The clear downside of having only one task origin is that it is a single point of failure. It worked in our favour because this was the first contest with a new scenario and the other teams didn't try to interfere too much with agents from the opposing team.

4   Match Analysis

In this section we analyse all of our matches in the 2019 MAPC. There were a total of four participating teams: Liverpool Formidable Constructors (LFC), FIT BUT, TRG, and GOAL-DTU. Each team used a different programming language (respectively): JaCaMo, Java, Jason, and GOAL. In total, our team won seven simulation rounds, had one draw, and lost one. With these results, we achieved a total of 22 points (3 per win, 1 per drawn, 0 per loss) and got the first place in the contest (7 points ahead of the second team, FIT BUT).

In Table 1, we show the total score obtained by each team. The total score is the sum of the score obtained from successfully delivering tasks across all rounds. The highest score in a single round was achieved by team FIT BUT, with a score of 680. In that particular round, their agents managed to deliver several tasks of size three (i.e., three attached blocks). Although TRG generated more overall score than GOAL-DTU, their final placement is lower (fourth place) since they only won one round in contrast with the three wins from GOAL-DTU.

Table 1. Total score of each team.

Team	Total score
LFC	1790
FIT BUT	1760
TRG	590
GOAL-DTU	330

Due to the inherent randomness of this year's scenario, we are not able to do direct comparisons between rounds 1, 2, and 3, in each of the matches since the map in a round can be completely different in the same round of another match.

4.1 LFC vs FIT BUT

Our first match was against FIT BUT and it was decisive in determining the winner of the contest. Although FIT BUT performed very well against the other teams, achieving a total score in delivered tasks similar to ours, they were not able to complete any tasks (except for one in the third round) against our team. Our agents did not (intentionally) try to sabotage the opponents in any of our matches. After a task is successfully delivered or if it fails, our origin agent tries to clear any visible cell within its vision radius of any blocks/obstacles. All agents will also perform a similar clear if they reconnect to a match (due to latency or deadlocks). We cleared some of the blocks from FIT BUT agents in this way, however, it is difficult to ascertain if that is what influenced our victories in any of the three rounds.

During the first match, we noticed a bug that would occur after successfully delivering a task where the origin agent would (sometimes) send no action for several steps. Occasionally the agent was able to recover from it by itself after a few steps, otherwise we had to manually reconnect all agents. This had a severe impact on the amount of tasks we could complete in the round, since after a reconnect our team started from scratch. We believed the source of this bug was the strategy for failure recovery that we added in the last few days before the contest. After the match, we decided to disable this feature for future matches. This did not have the desired impact, as the bug still occurred and our team was not able to automatically recover from failure in the remaining matches.

4.2 LFC vs TRG

We won the first and the third round and had a draw in the second round against TRG. TRG observable tactics consisted in splitting the agents into two groups. One focused on solving the tasks, and the other one (majority) focused on patrolling goal clusters (possibly to stop the other team from completing tasks). The agents belonging to the latter occupied the goal positions not used by they teammates, and they kept patrolling these areas clearing all the blocks in their vision.

In the first round, our team quickly achieved a score of 180 by step 256 (out of 500), which was our final score in that round. Due to pre-existing blocks close to the origin position, one of our agents that was bringing a block to the origin got stuck in a movement loop. Since we removed failure recovery after the previous match against FIT BUT, our agents never recovered. Although we were watching the matches live, we could only see the results of each agent's action, and thus did not notice the bug. We could have easily lost/tied the round due to this bug, since TRG performed very well and their agents were still completing tasks after our agents stopped. The third round was very similar to the first, except this time we noticed the bug and tried to reconnect the agents. Unfortunately, they were not able to deliver any tasks after reconnecting, however, we already had a good lead over TRG, enough to secure our win in that round.

In the second round, the patrolling TRG agents picked the goal cluster that our agents selected to deliver tasks. Thus, each time our agents tried to complete a task, their agents cleared the blocks attached to our origin agent, causing our agents to fail. Since we disabled automatic failure recovery, we were unable to deliver any tasks in this round. Luckily, TRG also did not manage to deliver any tasks, thus the round ended in a draw. This round was a good example of our single point of failure, the origin agent. Since we only use one goal cluster, if this cluster is disputed in any way, our team fails and is not able to properly recover from it. Future extensions should consider using multiple origin agents or having dynamic movement between different clusters.

4.3   LFC vs GOAL-DTU

GOAL-DTU is the only team to which we have lost a round. Specifically, in the second round GOAL-DTU won by 130 to 40, while our team won rounds one and three by a good margin. By observing the match against GOAL-DTU, we noticed the following behaviour. First, their agents explore the map to collect as many blocks as possible (i.e., each agent collects four blocks). Second, as soon as the agents agree on a task, then those involved in the task detach from unnecessary blocks, and move with the only remaining block into a goal position. Finally, the agents try to assemble and to submit the task. As any strategy, the one adopted by GOAL-DTU has advantages and disadvantages. On one side, their strategy seems to be rather resilient to potential attacks by other teams since the goal position is established only at the time of completing a task and each agent carries multiple blocks. On the other hand, having all the agents moving around with four blocks attached to them is not trivial. For example, in the replay of round one around step 305 agent $G5$ collects four blocks, but then it is unable to move away from the dispenser because the attached blocks collide with surrounding obstacles and it is stuck on a loop for the remaining of the round. This is why we decided that our agents would only move with one attached block.

Round one and three had the same score and played very similar. We won both of them with a resulting score of 380 to 40. Our performance in both rounds were a result of the limited interaction between agents of different teams (i.e., for the most part there was no conflict in goal clusters), and a faster task execution by LFC after the exploration phase.

Round two, however, is more interesting to analyse because weaknesses of our approach were clearly shown. In such round, our team scored 40 points and we had to reconnect the agents twice. A reconnect means that all knowledge acquired by the agents is lost, and all agents resume the initial strategy of exploring the map after clearing the surrounding area. The first reset happens at step 190, when we realised that agent $L6$ was stuck in a loop. The loop was caused by the enemy agent *G9* being in the cell which *L6* consider its destination. This resulted in agent *L6* moving back and forth hoping for a change in the situation (e.g., that *G9* would move to a different cell). As agent *L6* was crucial for the completion of the task, and the situation was not changing, we opted to reconnect our agents. After the first reconnect, it took almost 100 steps for the agents to gather enough information and stop their exploration. The agents behaved as expected until a clear event at step 304 occurred. The event resulted in our origin to be disabled, making any attempt of fulfilling a task unsuccessful. It took us about 100 steps before recognising the problem, and the second restart of the agents occurred at step 408, which was clearly too late for our agents to recover from the score disadvantage, resulting in our only loss in the contest.

5   Team Overview: Short Answers

5.1   Participants and Their Background

What was your motivation to participate in the contest?
The new scenario introduced this year was our main motivation, since it required a fresh start and a new perspective to solve it due to the additional randomness of its grid environment. We also wanted to improve our knowledge about agent technologies, and put them into practice in a complex multi-agent scenario.

What is the history of your group? (course project, thesis, ...)
All members of our group are post-doctoral research associates at the University of Liverpool.

What is your field of research? Which work therein is related?
Our work at the moment mostly relates to formal verification. We have not formally verified any aspect of our implementation yet, however there are several things that could be interesting to verify, such as our protocol to merge the maps, the individual planning of the agents, etc.

5.2   Statistics

How much time did you invest in the contest (for programming, organizing your group, other)?
Approximately 200 h.

How many lines of code did you produce for your final agent team?
A total of 6,783 lines of code, with 1,369 in Java and 5,414 in Jason.

How many people were involved?
Three post-docs:

Rafael C. Cardoso (PhD, Postdoctoral Research Associate at University of Liverpool)

Angelo Ferrando (PhD, Postdoctoral Research Associate at University of Liverpool)

Fabio Papacchini (PhD, Postdoctoral Research Associate at University of Liverpool)

When did you start working on your agents?

Our first commit to our online repository was on May 8th, 2019. However, most of the work started on September and continued up to the day of the contest.

5.3   Agent System Details

How does the team work together? (i.e. coordination, information sharing, ...) How decentralised is your approach?

Our agents start completely decentralised, each with their own local map. As the agents meet each other, they start merging their information. When evaluating tasks and assembling a team, our solution is centralised, as only the agent in the origin goal position can do so.

Do your agents make use of the following features: Planning, Learning, Organisations, Norms? If so, please elaborate briefly.

Each agent uses an instance of an automated planner (Fast Downward) to plan its movement using only its local vision. If the target position is outside of its local vision, the agent picks the closest position inside its vision and plan a path to go there, once it arrives it loops until arriving at the desired target position.

Can your agents change their behavior during runtime? If so, what triggers the changes?

Initially all agents are explorers, but when enough agents meet each other and enough dispensers and goal positions are known, then agents start to migrate to different roles, such as goal origin, block retriever, etc.

Did you have to make changes to the team (e.g. fix critical bugs) during the contest?

Close to the start of the first match we noticed that we had a bug where after completing a task the origin agent would die (i.e. send no action) for a few steps. We couldn't change anything in time for the first match, but we tried fixing it while the match was underway. Unfortunately, our changes ended up making our team worse and not fixing the bug.

How did you go about debugging your system?

Unfortunately JaCaMo does not have good debugging features yet, thus we used prints to test that critical parts of our code were behaving as intended.

During the contest you were not allowed to watch the matches. How did you understand what your team of agents was doing? Did this understanding help you to improve your team's performance?

We were only able to see when one of our agents died (i.e. sent no action), but without the map it was difficult to understand the context of the problem. For example, during one of the matches we noticed (via prints) that one of our agents was stuck in a loop, however, we were not able to tell if this agent was involved in performing a task or not. Without this knowledge, we decided to reconnect all agents, which is very costly as they start from zero.

Did you invest time in making your agents more robust? How?

Only very close to the day of the contest did we add task failure recovery and automated round change, until then we were improving our main strategies. This is probably what caused most bugs, since we did not have time to test it properly.

5.4 Scenario and Strategy

What is the main strategy of your agent team?

Our main strategy is twofold: first we build a consistent map that can be used by all agents to speed up the achievement of new tasks; then we move smartly using an automated planner.

Your agents only got local perceptions of the whole scenario. Did your agents try to build a global view of the scenario for a specific purpose? If so, describe it briefly.

Our agents merge their local maps when they meet a new agent. This map contains limited information: the coordinates of dispensers and goal positions. Each agent maintains its own position in the current map up to date, but this is not shared unless specifically requested by another agent.

How do your agents decide which tasks to complete?

An agent moves to a scouted origin position (must be a goal position). Once in position, this agent evaluates any new task to check if there are enough agents in place (nearby the origin) with the correct block types for the task.

Do your agents form ad-hoc teams to complete a task?

The team is formed by the origin agent, the other agents simply receive a subtask to bring their block to a particular position.

Which aspect(s) of the scenario did you find particularly challenging?

A major barrier at the start was the lack of shared information between the agents. Since each agent had its own local vision, we had to come up with a solution so that agents could identify each other when they met, and then exchange information to start building a shared map. Another challenge was to deal with the dynamic clear events coming from the environment, as these could create/remove obstacles and erase blocks that our agents were using to complete a task.

If another developer needs to integrate your techniques into their code (i.e., same programming language tools), how easy is it to make that integration work?

If the same programming language is used (JaCaMo) then it should be easy to add some of our techniques, due to the modularity of our solution.

5.5 And the Moral of It Is ...

What did you learn from participating in the contest?

Combining classical automated planning with agents is not as slow as we thought it would be. Of course the problem had to be reduced to include only the local vision of the agent, but given the timeout of 4 s, we were surprised that all 10 agents were able to plan concurrently in the same step.

What are the strong and weak points of your team?

The strong points of our team are the map merging techniques and the individual path planning. Our weak point is that we only have one agent in an origin goal position, so if something goes wrong with it we are unable to complete tasks.

Where did you benefit from your chosen programming language, methodology, tools, and algorithms?

We used the JaCaMo development platform, a combination of Jason, CArtAgO, and Moise. We benefited from the modularity and the many internal actions available in Jason. CArtAgO helped us interface with the server and share common knowledge between our agents. We did not use Moise, but we hope to do so next year.

Which problems did you encounter because of your chosen technologies?

Debugging a platform that uses multiple technologies is complicated. Most of our tests had to be done by adding prints in several places we wanted to test.

Did you encounter new problems during the contest?

We encountered several problems. The most troublesome was that after delivering a task the origin agent would die (i.e. send no action) for a few steps. While trying to fix this problem we deactivated things such as failure recovery from the second match forward. This made our team worse and did not fix the problem.

Did playing against other agent teams bring about new insights on your own agents?

There were many interesting strategies used by other teams. TRG had a team of disruptive agents that would keep moving in a goal cluster. GOAL-DTU made use of all four sides of an agent to connect four blocks. FIT BUT agents would meet with complex block structures and assemble it close to a goal cluster, then after the structure was complete they would move in a goal position to deliver.

What would you improve (wrt. your agents) if you wanted to participate in the same contest a week from now (or next year)?

We would make use of Moise, since most problems we had were related to coordination between agents, something that Moise organisations excels at.

Which aspect of your team cost you the most time?

We had long discussions about how to merge maps effectively, and the planning component took some time to integrate with the agents.

What can be improved regarding the contest/scenario for next year?

I think longer matches would be better. While 500 steps make it faster to play, I think they were too short to really display the best characteristics of each team. Having more agents per team will also enable more interesting strategies. Finally, it would be interesting to have actions that could interact/interfere with agents of the opposing team.

Why did your team perform as it did? Why did the other teams perform better/worse than you did?

We believe our success was due to the combination of: our agent identification, map merging, task coordination, and movement using an automated planner. Due to our centralised solution in solving tasks, our team was very vulnerable to any attempt that would disrupt our agent in the goal origin. Luckily, the other teams were also focused on solving the tasks.

6 Conclusion

In this paper we have described the tools and strategies used by our team (LFC) to win the 2019 MAPC. Our main contribution is the integration of JaCaMo agents with the Fast Downward planner. Although the four second deadline per step can often restrict the techniques used, we were able to workaround this limitation by reducing the state space that the planner had to search, while still allowing each agent to call its own instance of the planner without surpassing the deadline. Our strategies for constructing a global map (including exploration and agent identification) and achieving tasks (including choosing a goal position, retrieving blocks, and assembling block structures) were also crucial in achieving our results.

Since the number of agents per team will likely increase for the next contest, we would like to improve the interaction between agent and planner to be less computationally demanding. Another important improvement would be to revamp the model of the problem that is translated from the agent's knowledge and given as input to the planner to include more details about the environment. Future iterations of our team should also make use of Moise to program a role-based organisation and to implement proper coordination among agents.

References

1. Ahlbrecht, T., Dix, J., Fiekas, N.: The multi-agent programming contest - a résumé. In: Ahlbrecht, T., et al. (eds.) MAPC 2019. LNAI, vol. 12381, pp. 3–27. Springer, Cham (2020)
2. Boissier, O., Bordini, R.H., Hübner, J.F., Ricci, A., Santi, A.: Multi-agent oriented programming with JaCaMo. Sci. Comput. Program. **78**(6), 747–761 (2013). https://doi.org/10.1016/j.scico.2011.10.004. ISSN: 0167-6423
3. Bordini, R.H., Hübner, J.F., Wooldridge, M.: Programming Multi-Agent Systems in AgentSpeak Using Jason. Wiley, Hoboken (2007)
4. Cardoso, R.C., Krausburg, T., Baségio, T., Engelmann, D.C., Hübner, J.F., Bordini, R.H.: SMART-JaCaMo: an organization-based team for the multi-agent programming contest. Ann. Math. Artif. Intell. **84**(1), 75–93 (2018). https://doi.org/10.1007/s10472-018-9584-z
5. Cardoso, R.C., Pereira, R.F., Krzisch, G., Magnaguagno, M.C., Baségio, T., Meneguzzi, F.: Team PUCRS: a decentralised multi-agent solution for the agents in the city scenario. Int. J. Agent-Oriented Softw. Eng. **6**(1), 3–34 (2018). https://doi.org/10.1504/IJAOSE.2018.10010601
6. Helmert, M.: The fast downward planning system. J. Artif. Intell. Res. **26**, 191–246 (2006). https://doi.org/10.1613/jair.1705
7. Helmert, M.: Concise finite-domain representations for PDDL planning tasks. Artif. Intell. **173**(5–6), 503–535 (2009). https://doi.org/10.1016/j.artint.2008.10.013

 8. Hübner, J.F., Sichman, J.S., Boissier, O.: Developing organised multiagent systems using the MOISE+ model: programming issues at the system and agent levels. Int. J. Agent-Oriented Softw. Eng. **1**(3/4), 370–395 (2007)
 9. Krausburg, T., et al.: SMART–JaCaMo: an organisation-based team for the multi-agent programming contest. In: Ahlbrecht, T., Dix, J., Fiekas, N. (eds.) MAPC 2018. LNCS (LNAI), vol. 11957, pp. 72–100. Springer, Cham (2019). https://doi.org/10.1007/978-3-030-37959-9_4
10. Mcdermott, D., et al.: PDDL - the planning domain definition language. Technical report TR-98-003, Yale Center for Computational Vision and Control (1998)
11. Rao, A.S., Georgeff, M.P.: Modeling rational agents within a BDI-architecture. In: Allen, J., Fikes, R., Sandewall, E. (eds.) Proceedings of the 2nd International Conference on Principles of Knowledge Representation and Reasoning, pp. 473–484. Morgan Kaufmann publishers Inc., San Mateo (1991)
12. Ricci, A., Piunti, M., Viroli, M., Omicini, A.: Environment programming in CArtAgO. In: El Fallah Seghrouchni, A., Dix, J., Dastani, M., Bordini, R.H. (eds.) Multi-Agent Programming, pp. 259–288. Springer, Boston, MA (2009). https://doi.org/10.1007/978-0-387-89299-3_8

Multi-Agent Programming Contest 2019 FIT BUT Team Solution

Vaclav Uhlir$^{(\boxtimes)}$ (ID), Frantisek Zboril (ID), and Frantisek Vidensky (ID)

Department of Intelligent Systems, Faculty of Information Technology,
Brno University of Technology, Brno, Czech Republic
{iuhlir,zborilf,ividensky}@fit.vutbr.cz
https://www.fit.vut.cz/.en

Abstract. During our participation in MAPC 2019, we have developed two multi-agent systems that have been designed specifically for this competition. The first of the systems is a proactive system that works with pre-specified scenarios and tasks agents with generated goals designed for individual agents according to assigned role. The second system is designed as more reactive and employs layered architecture with highly dynamic behaviour, where agents select their own action based on their perception of usefulness of said action.

Keywords: Artificial intelligence · Multi-Agent Programming · Decision-making planning · Self-organisation

1 Introduction

This paper describes our first participation in Multi-Agent Programming Contest 2019 (MAPC). The main motivation for our participation was to compare our skill in implementing logic in multi-agent systems and try various approaches. Specifically, this text will describe two systems which we implemented for this contest – where the first one, named "deSouches" (Sect. 2), was used for qualification and second one, named "FIT BUT" (Sect. 3), was used for the main competition.

1.1 MAPC 2019 Environment

This year, the assignment of the MAPC competition follows the story of robots that have to assemble and deliver specific structures from various blocks. For almost a decade, robotic agents have been on Mars, then on Earth, and now they are back on Mars and have to deal with an unstable volcanic environment [10].

From the classical point of view [1] we may classify such environment as non-accessible, discrete, dynamic, non-deterministic, sequential and social. A non-accessible and partially observable environment provides agents with limited object visibility - where agents have limited vision to certain distance. This distance is fortunately known at the runtime and also unchanging and same for

© Springer Nature Switzerland AG 2020
T. Ahlbrecht et al. (Eds.): MAPC 2019, LNAI 12381, pp. 59–78, 2020.
https://doi.org/10.1007/978-3-030-59299-8_3

all agents during whole simulation. Agents also have limited recognition capabilities allowing them to recognize friend or foe, but not other characteristics (i.e. name or id of the seen agent). On the other hand, agents have no limitation on communication. They are able to communicate freely and thus use shared knowledge allowing them to construct and manage shared map and use it to synchronize their actions.

1.2   DeSouches and FIT BUT Team at MAPC 2019

Two systems that we developed for the MAPC 2019 differs in approach and aim. The first one, "deSouches", was a multi-agent system which proactively performed specific scenarios, and we used it for qualification. Then, thanks to the extended time between qualification and the competition, we modified the first one to a more reactive form and because the second system was performing slightly better than the first one, we used the latter in the main contest. The main goal of the competition is earning points and achieving a higher score than opponent in the current competition round. Points are earned by completing and submitting structures from found or requested special blocks scattered around the map thus requiring agents to search, assemble and deliver. The contest environment is generated at the start of the simulation and unknown to the agents and also dynamic through environment changing events. The environment is represented by a grid world containing obstacles, dispensers (places where blocks are issued) and goal marks - places where agents have to place assembled shapes.

Due to the design of competition simulation – agents are required to be able to actively cooperate with each other in the process of assembling structures. As a minimum for agents trying to join two blocks is active assistance of another agent from the same team. Other tasks, such as searching, delivering, clearing terrain or even targeted malicious action do not require team cooperation/synchronization but may provide a clear advantage when implemented.

2   deSouches Multi-agent System

The first problem addressed was the question of which architecture, language, implementation system, and multi-agent methods would be used for successful implementation of desired methods. We evaluated a number of solutions that were possibly suitable both for the implementation of a rational agent and for the use of multi-agent methodologies for teamwork or conflict resolution. Among the most important was JASON [2], which interprets the language AgentSpeak (L) [3] and, together with 2APL [5], is probably the best-known representative of systems that work on the basis of the BDI paradigm [4]. Extending JASON to JaCaMo [7] is a workable way to create multi-agent assemblies that pursue common goals and this would certainly be appropriate for creating systems for MAPC as this was successfully implemented by authors over the past seasons.

But as this year was a completely new scenario, we decided to try to use our experience with agents and a multi-agent system and create our own multi-agent system.

We decided to do the brand-new system that would fit the contest scenario and to implement it in JAVA. The reasons were rather intuitive. Beside an opportunity to try to make an agent system from scratch we had doubts about performance of today's agent systems in such a highly dynamic environment. We realized that it would be better to spent more time in implementation but to have the performance of the system under our own control. Finally we saw that this enabled us to change architecture of the system in quite short time to more reactive allowing improved behaviour of the agents, as we found out by comparison of the original and latter version.

The first architecture was made for the purposes of qualification. It was inspired by the BDI solutions mentioned above, but this system was more proactive with persistent goals rather than regular BDI system. In the following lines, we will describe this first system and in Sect. 3 we will present the modified system that we used during the main content.

2.1 General deSouches and His Soldiers

It is clear that the competition assignment was created, among other things, to verify the social ability of a multi-agent population in a dynamic and non-deterministic environment. It addressed the ability of agents to make a coalition and jointly follow a goal. This is still an ongoing issue in multi-agent systems and each team has to address this problem.

The first multi-agent system we named after a general who successfully commanded Brno's defence force against the siege of the Swedish army during the Thirty Years' War in 1645. We formed a group of agents in a very simple hierarchy where one agent – deSouches assumed commanding of others. The commands were in the form of scenarios that the soldier had to adopt. The soldiers then followed the scenario as they got goals that they should complete. Soldiers also informed deSouches when they successfully finished the scenario or when they failed to complete the scenario or simply that they needed a job.

2.2 Agent Level Architecture

Originally, our first agent architecture was designed to be one that works with a set of intentions. The intentions were created for a persistent goal and the agents build a hierarchy of procedural goals [6] and corresponding plans that should lead to the main intention goal achievement. But in the process of development, we ended up with a system where agents could contain only one intention and also the intention contained every time only the main goal. Thus the agent was driven by procedural goals that were represented by a goal class that includes methods for making a plan for the goal and processing of one action of an actual plan. Agent's beliefs about the environment consisted of a map of the environment and other information that it may get from its percepts – agent's own name, team name, energy and blocks in visible vicinity. The last contains the agent and all the attached blocks.

A plan is made from actions available to the agents according to the contest specification. An agent may traverse the environment, make clearing actions, attach, detach and connect blocks, rotate and submit tasks. Essential for our agent was that for selection of goals it could use A* search algorithm. In this case, it was slightly modified with the restriction of the number of iteration it could make. It was often impossible in a given map to get from one place to another, especially when the agent's body contained one or more blocks. Then the A* was unsuccessful and the planning for a goal failed.

Interpretation cycle was implemented as commonly expected – that is as it consisted of reasoning and execution parts –. During the reasoning part, the agent firstly processed its percepts then evaluated feedback from previously executed action (as it could have failed in the environment) and sent actual tasks proposed by the system to deSouches. Then agent took its intention, respectively the goal within the intention, reconsidered the plan for the goal and then executed one action of the plan.

2.3   Goals

There were about ten different goals that were specifically implemented for our agents. The agent has a choice of adopting a goal of traversal to a specific position. Or the goal of traversal where the agent would walk randomly to some specified distance. Several goals were related to the spacial manipulation of the blocks, block retrieval or to attachment and detachment of the blocks and finally to submitting blocks in a given direction. The last-mentioned goals were quite simple and the plans contained only a few actions, usually to rotate to the given direction and to attach, detach or submit a block.

2.4   Synchronization of Agent Groups

Because the agents do not know their absolute position on the environment grid they are also unable to deduct their relative positions to each other. If one agent discovers an obstacle, dispenser or block, other agents are not able to simply calculate their relative position to discovered object. Thus synchronization of agent positions was essential for successful behaviour of our agents. Our key idea for such synchronization is that when there is only one pair of agents that one agent sees friendly agent relatively to it on dx, dy and another agent sees friendly agent on $-dx$, $-dy$, then these two agents see one another and may synchronize. This will be described in more details further in the Sect. 3.2 in part of our second multi-agent system. Furthermore, we form agent groups that contain synchronized agents. At the beginning, we start with n groups for n agents. When there is a pair of agents that may be synchronized and these two agents are from different groups then we will join these groups together and merge their maps with respect to the shift vector between the pair of just synchronized agents. Consequently, we build up larger and larger groups and we can see that at most after $n - 1$ synchronizations there remains only one group containing all the agents and then our whole team is fully synchronized.

2.5 Scenarios

Scenarios are the main source of the behaviour of deSouches's agents in the game. Scenarios are in fact finite-state automatons by which the goals are assigned to agents. There is one automaton for every role in the scenario and as the goals are successfully or even unsuccessfully performed the automaton may change its state and assign another goal. When all the agents reach the final states then the scenario is completed and deSouches is informed. It may also happen that the scenario cannot be completed, for example when the deadline for a task is over and then deSouches is again informed with this fact.

There are three basic kinds of scenarios in our system. In the beginning, the agents need to explore the environment and get synchronized. After they are fully synchronized they will either work on a task or try to clear an area important for the team. A subgroup of agents may also be chosen for a task before the multiagent population is fully synchronized. Such a group must have number of agents equal or greater than the number of block needed and also beliefs where particular depots for needed types of blocks are. When deSouches creates a group of agent for a task, then such agents must try to complete the task. Before we will introduce the scenario we have to discuss the problem of synchronisation of agents in the environment.

Walk and synchronize scenario is the starting point for every agent. Exploring the map is achieved by soldiers that walk randomly in order to explore the map of the environment and also to synchronize the agents that are meeting while traversing the unknown environment. We will describe the synchronization later in this text. An agent that is supposed to walk randomly has to select a direction and with a distance in pre-specified range it chooses a point where it should go. Then it computes path using $A*$ algorithm, which is modified in such a way that the number of iterations is limited by a specific number (2500 proved to be adequate). This guarantees that it ends in sufficient time and also that it ends even when there does not exist a path to the destination. In either case, the agent follows the computed path returned by the algorithm. After it encounters an unexpected obstacle or finishes successfully given steps, the scenario is over and the agent sends corresponding (success/fail) message to deSouches. In the next step, deSouches sends back a new order to repeat this scenario in a new variant again or assigns the following search and destroy scenario.

Search and destroy scenario is ordered to agents after there is only one group of agents, this means that all of the agents are synchronized. In this case, the agents should be aware of where are the obstacles that need to be destroyed and if they can successfully reach them, then they try to destroy them by the clear actions. When they cannot get to the chosen obstacle or they do not have enough power to destroy it they report a failure to deSouches. Otherwise, after successful completion of this scenario, they report success to the general deSouches.

This scenario offers several alternative strategies on how to choose an obstacle for elimination. We considered that the agent could try to remove obstacles around the goal areas or dispensers. But in the resulting algorithm in the finished development stage of deSouches architecture the agents just take the nearest obstacles they can see and clear them.

Blocks scenarios are derived from the same class and are predefined for two, three and four blocks. For each of them, there is one master agent and one, two or three lieutenants. DeSouches, when discovers a possibility of fulfilling of a selected task and has available "mastergroup" that has more free agents than is required number for two, three respective four-block scenario – meaning at least two, three or four agents, initializes such scenario. Through this initialization, deSouches selects suitable agents from the mastergroup.

In case when there is no mastergroup yet, deSouches looks if there is a group that knows the position of all demanded dispenser types for the given task and also if there are enough number of unemployed agents in the group. If there is such a group, deSouches employs agents from this group for the tasks and the group also becomes a mastergroup. Once labelled as mastergroup the group remains mastergroup for the rest of the simulation run. During any further synchronizations, any other group will be synchronized with this group.

The agents have individual roles in this scenario. For every block scenarios, one agent is set as commander and one as the first lieutenant. For a three-block scenario, there is also the second lieutenant and for four block scenario, there is another – the third lieutenant. Commander would be finally responsible for submitting the task and we present the corresponding automaton for this role in this scenario in Fig. 1.

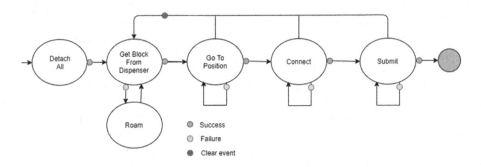

Fig. 1. Automaton for deSouches blocks scenario.

For lieutenants, the diagram is mostly the same except for the Submit goal – which is in this case omitted.

Each participant knows which type of block it should obtain and how to connect them. More specifically each agent in his role knows with which type and on what position in or nearby a selected goal cell he should stand (only the commander must stand on a goal cell). Agents also know the direction of their block must face before they will try to connect them together.

The blocks scenarios will use one of in total 42 plans that the agents are able to make in our system. This allows agents to plan and execute two, three and four block shapes assembles and submit scenarios.

There are three plans for shapes consisting of two blocks, ten plans for three-block shapes and the remaining twenty nine plans are for structures that are created from four blocks. In this agent implementation, we programmed them by enumeration instead of developing an algorithm that would generate such plans dynamically, as was originally intended at the very beginning of development.

Every agent in the team must know which type of block it should acquire and which position around the goal area it must take before it tries to connect the block in a given direction. If an agent manages to get the proper block then it tries to get to its goal position and then to connect the block with its teammates. If any plan goals fail then it tries to reach it again except the 'go to dispenser' goal where the agents try to perform a random traversal first before trying to achieve the agents intended original goal. Also if a clear event is fully performed on agent and results in loss of the block – agents must restart the scenario from the 'dispenser' goal again. When all the blocks are properly connected, all the agents except the commander detach their blocks and then the commander submits the task.

If every agent is able to complete successfully their automatons then the scenario should be successfully completed and the playing team should receive points for simulation task completion. The scenario may also fail when the task deadline lapses and in such case, general deSouches disbands the team and gives new orders to the agents – to perform another scenario.

3   FIT BUT System

The second system that we used for the final contest is named simply FIT BUT. In some parts, it overlaps with deSouches system (as it was built on its bases), but it is more reactive using a hierarchically layered model of behaviours and it is rather similar to Subsumption architecture [8] than the previous system was. After we compared both systems we found out that more reactivity instead of proactivity gives in such a dynamic environment as the MAPC 2019 better outcomes and for this reason we used FIT BUT for the main competition.

3.1   Design

Basic system flow can be seen in Fig. 2 and consists of three levels of granularity. The logical structure of the system is again hierarchical and agent units, supplied by system percepts are organized into population groups. Each such a group is then registered into global Register implemented by singleton class.

At the start of every step, agents evaluate their percepts and then contact Register class. After every agent successfully registers completion of percepts evaluation, Register – if needed – assigns agents to their new group (if new relative positions are confirmed) and contacts all groups and triggers groups calculation of agent options. Groups are informing agents upon every successful action option generation and it is left to the agents to select their future action, but it still has to be confirmed by the group reservation system. Upon successful confirmation, the agent in question returns desired action to simulation or if a reservation was unsuccessful has to find different action which will be confirmed by the group reservation system.

Every plan generated in this system contains a full set of actions following a purpose to the specified goal. But at every step in this system the old plan is replaced by a new plan influenced by environmental changes, thus only one (the first) action from every plan is ever used. This ensures fully reactive behavior and also allows clear tools for behavioral analysis.

3.2   Synchronization

The key features defining agent synchronization are agent *visibility, communi-cation capabilities* and *certainty*. We discussed the environment briefly at the beginning of this text. The main issue was that agents do not know the disposi-tion of their environment or starting position in relation to global map or to each other – but all agents have same orientation sense and most actions produce new determined position – either successfully executing (non)movement action with a new expected position, or getting action error with position unchanged. An Agent can reach (in his view) unexpected position by being dragged by another friendly agent in case where two agents are connected via blocks to the same total structure. This behavior can be eliminated by carefully monitoring agents block attachments and restricting movement actions while more agents are connected to the same structure.

As mentioned at the beginning of this text, the agents are not able to rec-ognize other agents in their vision beyond friend or foe. Fortunately, this is not the case in communication and messages can be signed and trusted allowing agents to compare their vision results. Due to the non-observable and dynamic environment using landscape recognition does not produce certain results with possible exception based on the border mapping by movement actions error log-ging. This process may be lengthy and in a highly dynamic environment nearly impossible as borders may not be reachable in meaningful time.   Based on these condition FIT BUT agents use position synchronization by implementing two-way confirmation solely based on seeing each other. This can be trusted as synchronization procedure in case of exactly two agents seeing another agent at the same distance but in opposite direction and if no other agents detect any other agent in the same distance and direction (Fig. 3) these two agents can be certain of their current relative position difference and with successful tracking of their own action they can determine their position relation for the rest of the simulation.

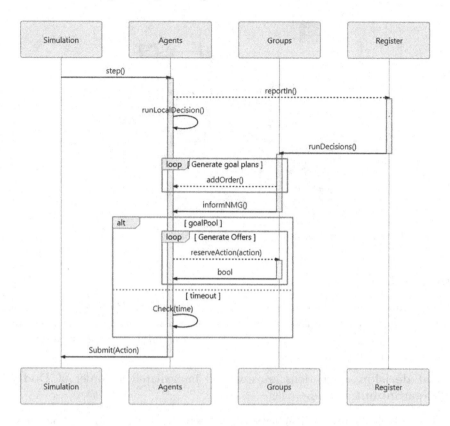

Fig. 2. Overview of one step in FIT BUT system.

3.3   FIT BUT Agent Reasoning Cycle

FIT BUT system works on bases of options calculation that the agents try to discover during their interpretation cycle. Due to the limitations of resources [9], especially time constraints, not every option may be discovered. Discovered options are formed into the possible plans which are sorted based on priorities and resources availability with the aim of maximizing points. In every agent step, only the first action of the plan for the option with the highest priority is executed and in the following step, the agent computes its options again. Thanks to this approach, the agent is very reactive and careful because it reconsiders its behaviour in every cycle. Below we will specify these phases in more detail.

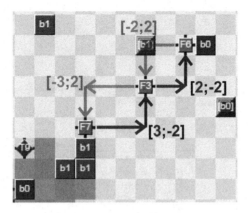

Fig. 3. Example of using distance difference for agent recognition.

3.4   Options Analysis

After agents evaluate their perception both local and group decisions calculations are triggered simultaneously and in order as seen in Fig. 4. While calculating options, the watchdog is checking time and may terminate calculations if calculation should exceed current step timeout.

Local decision calculations are executed immediately in order of **Dodge**, **GoNearSubmit** and **Dig**, where:

- **Dodge** checks if any clear action is expected on agents (or his body part) position and if needed plots shortest escape course out of clear action influence area.
- **GoNearSubmit** finds nearest (currently seen or remembered) goal position and calculates a path to it.
- **Dig** plots path to the closest terrain and if the terrain block is in range triggers clear terrain action for such block.

The first locally analysed option **Dodge** is intended to protect agents integrity especially when carrying blocks. This action takes precedence over most other actions and has priority in the reservation system. Also when this action is present in possible actions stack, low priority actions may be excluded from the calculation. Remaining local actions **GoNearSubmit** and **Dig** are intended as fallback on group coordination problems and timeouts. Action **GoNearSubmit** is intended to bring agents close to submit areas to decrease their collective distance difference or enable discovery of other friendly agents. Remaining action **Dig** is executed as a last resort if no other action and thus no path to a goal area is found. This is intended for agents stuck inside terrain without known access to useful space.

Group decision options calculation is started when the last of the agents reports finished evaluating perceptions. As the calculation of group options may

Calculation of agent options

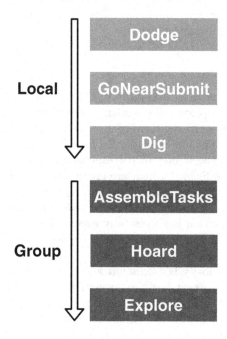

Fig. 4. Options discovery order.

be very resource-intensive – it is expected that not all of the options will be calculated and agents with priority plans already assigned are excluded from further options calculation. Group options discovery is performed in order of **AssembleTasks**, **Hoard** and **Explore**, where:

– **AssembleTasks** searches for blocks and paths for active tasks (detailed in Sect. 3.7).
– **Hoard** fetches and attaches blocks to the agent.
– **Explore** roams agent into unknown or longest unseen parts of the environment.

The first considered option: **AssembleTasks** is the one most resource-intensive, but most important in scoring points. This calculation is more resource heavy more block agents have hoarded and more space have they explored, so starving **Hoard** and **Explore** calculation is not as critical in such case and in case of no blocks hoarded or goals explored this action is entirely skipped.

Hoard action is intended for acquiring of blocks (either retrieving already existing blocks in the environment or obtaining block from the dispenser) and attaching them to the agent body.

The last group goal **Explore** aims at discovering new dispensers, blocks, goals and also other agents. Agents in cooperation group divide the unknown area into section and each agent tries to discover assigned part (usually closest to its position). If no unknown areas are accessible agents will perform a check of areas that are longest unseen (this is aimed to monitor terrain changes and find possible previously undiscovered areas).

3.5   Plan Selection

Every agent is selecting its plan for execution in the current step from the available plans created for the options discovered as described above in Sect. 3.4. Every option produces a plan in the form of an action stack where this actions correspond to the actions that are available for the agent in MAPC. Names of the plans are the same as the names of corresponding options with exception of plans *GoConnect* and *GoSubmit* which are created for the **AssembleTasks** option and the plan *Roam* that is created for the **Explore** option.

Furthermore, there may be also a plan named *Split* that was created immediately after a connection action is successfully executed and is persistent until agents are separated. Plan intended for execution is selected in priority order as shown in Fig. 5.

Plan with the highest priority is *GoSubmit* and is adopted when an agent is able to submit part of his current body as an active task requirement. If such action is not possible and the agent is still connected to another agent then the agent results in plan *Split*. This should eliminate unwanted position change by agents dragging each other by other movement actions.

Next in order is again *GoSubmit*, this time with limitation on its plan size – more precisely when the plan is less than 3 actions in length. Such a plan is preferred to the next option *–Dodge*. This is in line of reasoning that continuing of submission shall probably be finished before the clear action is performed and therefore advantageous. After plan option *Dodge* follows again plan *GoSubmit* this time without the additional limitations intended for execution of the rest of its variations.

If agent doesn't have task which it may submit and none of the above mentioned types of plans are available, then the agent follows with the selection in the order of *GoConnect*, *Hoard*, *Roam*, *GoNearSubmit* and *Dig*.

The reason for an agent to create new plans that will inevitably have lower priority than already created plans from previous options is to allow the agent to generate backup actions in a case where the agent may not be able to perform previously selected action with a higher priority. As mentioned above, the agent has to select a new plan in every interpretation cycle and from this plan agent will execute only the first action. To mitigate team collisions the agent has to check his action against the actions of his teammates and thus before action is executed it has to be confirmed by the system that no collision shall occur in cases of successful or even unsuccessful actions. This safety feature is performed by the action reservation system.

Selection of agent action

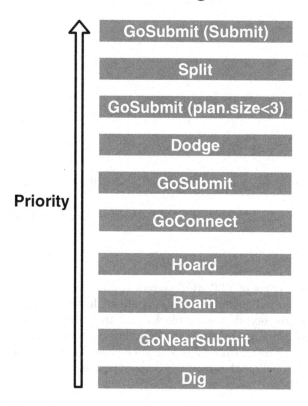

Fig. 5. Priority order of plan selection in which agent tries to execute selected operation.

3.6   Action Reservation System

As mentioned above all agents, when choosing an action for execution, must first contact reservation system (as can be seen in Fig. 2 with call *"reserveAction(..)"*) which creates a map of expected result for the next step and required free spaces for movement or action operations. This map is shared for all agents in the current synchronized group. Reservation system then can approve the agent action and reserve needed cells (or blocks or other resources) or can reject their action which results in agents having to submit different action for review. Successful reservation can be seen in log files from competition on Fig. 6 where (after successful structure joining and agents disconnecting) agent 7 wants to request a new block from dispenser bellow (Fig. 6a) and then agent 3 requests traverse movement to the right towards his goal (Fig. 6b) and thus resulting successful operations will change the environment from original step (Fig. 6c) to the next step (Fig. 6d).

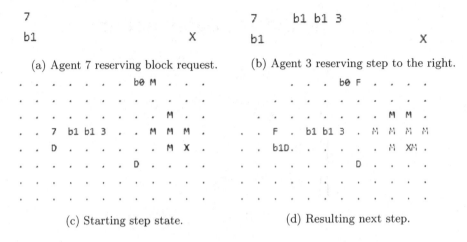

(a) Agent 7 reserving block request.   (b) Agent 3 reserving step to the right.

(c) Starting step state.   (d) Resulting next step.

Fig. 6. Successful reservation and execution of agents actions.

3.7 Task Possibilities Commutations

One of the crucial parts of FIT BUT system is finding suitable structures that may be used for assembling active tasks. Assembling has to be done by the agents (which have already hoarded some blocks and are still in possession of these blocks) and have to be performed by collaboration and following simultaneous joining call. Analysis on which structures shall be joined to achieve desired shapes and types is performed for the *AssembleTasks* option and is done algorithmically as described by the following steps:

1. Insert every agent to connection candidates set (CCS).
2. Evaluate currently held structures with active tasks, if any agent is already in possession of structure fitting to a requested task structure and the agent can plot a path to a goal area, then create a new *Submit* plan for such agent and remove it from the CCS.
3. Sort the structures carried by agents in order from most complete to least complete in regard to required tasks and their value.
4. For every active task and every agent in CCS, generate combinations of agent pairs and their structures fitting targeted tasks with respect to their order from the previous step. All generated combinations have to be connected and cannot overlap on any block.
5. Sort the generated structures by metric composed of steps needed for their assembly and reward for the corresponding active task.
6. While there is a pair of agents in CCS that were identified as suitable pair for any connection:
   - Select a generated structure with the highest metric value where both agents are in CCS.
   - Create for such agents corresponding *GoConnection* plans
   - Remove these agents from CCS.

Generating combination for every task, every agent and every block would be very resource-intensive and therefore sorting and option pool trimming is implemented on multiple points in the algorithm.

4 Limitations and Possible Improvements

Our agents are limited in lots of aspects due to planned but unimplemented features which could improve future potential.

4.1 Size Control

One of such features is structure size control – tool for checking size of the future connected structure against the system limit. For example, in testing matches the maximal size of the structure was set to 10 blocks. Let us suppose two agents with a connected block on their every side – connecting such entities would result in a structure with 8 blocks and 2 agents thus totaling 10 blocks and triggering the system limit.

4.2 Hoarding

Hoarding routine is implemented for connecting blocks to all of the sides of the agent but due to missing size control was limited to a maximum of one block, which proved useful enough for time being and other issues took precedents. Upon implementation of size control agents should benefit from faster block matching for all the tasks. The downside of enabling hoarding for more than 1 block is the limitation of agent movement capabilities as it would not be possible to manoeuvre through tight places and either dynamic block dropping or additional terrain digging may be required for maintaining agent mobility.

It should be noted that hoarding section of code contains function *isBlock-Interesting(BlockType)* intended for management of block type possession of the whole group. This function was not yet properly implemented and always returns *true*. While this missing functionality was fortunately not the issue during competition it poses the risk of agents not hoarding diverse enough blocks and thus limiting their capability to fulfill task (as current task possibilities are computed only from hoarded blocks and agents with hoarded wrong blocks can deadlock their assembly possibilities).

5 Conclusion

Both of our solutions described in this text were able to complete a number of given tasks in the MAPC 2019 game scenarios. As was described in Sects. 2.4 and 3.2 synchronization of the agents is one of the key aspects on road to success and necessity in such dynamic environment with agents having only limited vision capability and without information about their absolute position within a coordinate system. Another obstacle described and solved in the work above is problem of agents recognition – final solution of this problem is relatively simple, but as explained in Sect. 3.2 it is efficient enough and furthermore reliable without fault. Using this method our algorithms were able to form work groups.

The first described system named deSouches (Sect. 2), that was used for qualification, presented close multi-agent cooperation and assembling the tasks using agents from one synchronized group. Each agent from this group was assigned with retrieving and transporting one specific block for the chosen task. This block was transported to the goal area where all of the tasked agents connected them to the required shape and agent assigned as commander of the group submitted them for the specified reward.

The second described system, with assumed team name FIT BUT (Sect. 3), that was eventually used for MAPC competition was more reactive and used agents to collect blocks as an opportunity arose. Such collected blocks where then connected to form expected shapes or their sub-parts. Such sub-parts were formed opportunistically and without a set future plan, but thanks to constant reevaluating in every step this proved to be quite functional and mainly very robust when it came to overcoming environment events and enemy agents actions.

Both of the systems had their advantages and disadvantages – first one more constant in outcomes end with pre-planned goals proved to have higher base reliability. The second system was thanks to its reactivity far more versatile and dynamic, but with dangers of bottlenecking or encountering obscure problems in specific scenarios. Both of the systems proved their main required features in their respective competition rounds.

Acknowledgment. This work was supported by the project IT4IXS: IT4Innovations Excellence in Science project (LQ1602).

A   Team Overview: Short Answers

A.1   Participants and Their Background

What was your motivation to participate in the contest?
Our group is related to artificial agents and multi-agent systems and we wanted to compete in an international contest and test our skills.

What is the history of your group? (course project, thesis, ...)
Members of our research group have been teaching artificial intelligence at our faculty for nearly 20 years. Most of the projects or thesis in our group concern the topic of artificial intelligence, multi-agent systems, soft-computing and machine learning.

What is your field of research? Which work therein is related?
Vaclav Uhlir: Ecosystems involving autonomous units (mainly autonomous cars).
František Zboril and Frantisek Videnky: Artificial agents and BDI agents.

Frantisek Zboril's field of research is also prototyping of wireless sensor networks using mobile agents.

A.2   Statistics

How much time did you invest in the contest (for programming, organizing your group, other)?
Something between 200 to 300 hours of programming and another 100 of planning, strategizing and managing *git* and other development environments.
How many lines of code did you produce for your final agent team?
5531 lines of code.
797 comment lines.
42 active "TODO" in final code.
How many people were involved?
3
When did you start working on your agents?
Aug 29, 2019 10:41am.

A.3   Agent System Details

How does the team work together? (i.e. coordination, information sharing, ...) How decentralised is your approach?
Every agent has its local tasks with priority list as a fallback and if time allows, it waits for local group decision (triggered by the slowest agent in the group).
Do your agents make use of the following features: Planning, Learning, Organisations, Norms? If so, please elaborate briefly.
Our agents plan is only one step and agent are organized into groups as they "meet" - within these groups agents cooperate based on momentary advantage.
Can your agents change their behavior during runtime? If so, what triggers the changes?
Every action is dependent only on the current environment and few randomizers independent on previous steps.
Did you have to make changes to the team (e.g. fix critical bugs) during the contest?
Yes, we enabled not-fully-tested beta features hoping to achieve better error handling.
How did you go about debugging your system? Custom logger with 5 levels of logging for every agent and bound to various subsystems. (By average every contest match produced around 1 GB plain-text info.)
During the contest you were not allowed to watch the matches. How did you understand what your team of agents was doing? Did this understanding help you to improve your team's performance?
An overwhelming flood of error indicated network problems and resulted in agent desynchronization - limiting the system higher functions. Enabling beta features eliminated some network issues but introduced other errors.

Did you invest time in making your agents more robust? How?
Robustness was planned via fallback strategies – some of them were implemented in beta features, but most was not ready for the main contest.

A.4   Scenario and Strategy

What is the main strategy of your agent team?
Aiming for closest possible highly valued target while effectively ignoring past.
Your agents only got local perceptions of the whole scenario. Did your agents try to build a global view of the scenario for a specific purpose? If so, describe it briefly.
Upon successful position confirmation of any two agents, agents were assigned to workgroups synchronizing any new perception to the global map used in the search for highest achievable task completion.
How do your agents decide which tasks to complete?
When a task is available and all required blocks are accessible and their joining can result in the successful completion of structure and structure can be delivered to the goal. Task value selection is based on reward and the number of steps needed with a slight preference for smaller structures.
Do your agents form ad-hoc teams to complete a task?
Agents cooperate in team-like structures but in every step, the cooperation can be reevaluated.
Which aspect(s) of the scenario did you find particularly challenging?
Identification of block attachments (to each other or agents).
If another developer needs to integrate your techniques into their code (i.e., same programming language tools), how easy is it to make that integration work?
Definitely under average as some in-code named features are not fully complete and/or are using various temporal workarounds.

A.5   And the Moral of It Is . . .

What did you learn from participating in the contest?
Relatively simply looking scenario can present a far greater challenge than we expected.
What are the strong and weak points of your team?
Our team has expertise in multiple different languages and coding approach techniques.
Every member has specialization in different programming language and techniques.
Where did you benefit from your chosen programming language, methodology, tools, and algorithms?
Familiarity with the used environment allowed for faster development for some team members.

Which problems did you encounter because of your chosen technologies?
Mainly portability issues over different operating systems and conflicting environment variables.

Did you encounter new problems during the contest? Yes - battling environment and OS portability on large scale.

Did playing against other agent teams bring about new insights on your own agents? Yes - mainly highlighting strength and weaknesses and opening ideas for new strategies.

What would you improve (wrt. your agents) if you wanted to participate in the same contest a week from now (or next year)? Error handling, network code, fallback strategies - in this order.

Which aspect of your team cost you the most time? In the early versions of the system, we had a nasty bug that sometimes caused subsequent errors in synchronization amongst agents and problems in other systems. This was blamed on various other possible sources and caused very lengthy bug-hunting through multiple environments.

What can be improved regarding the contest/scenario for next year? Clarification about block connections - either changing perceptions with some sort of connection information or clear warning about the uncertainty of block connections.

Why did your team perform as it did? Why did the other teams perform better/worse than you did?
Our agents were running on a machine with desynchronized clock (about $-3.5\,\mathrm{s}$) and thus fearing timeouts, agents were submitting action prematurely with less than $0.5\,\mathrm{s}$ on decisions - which they were not built for and because of this the higher system planning was often not effectively used.

References

1. Russell, S., Norvig, P.: Artificial Intelligence: A Modern Approach. Prentice Hall, Upper Saddle River (2010)
2. Bordini, R.H., Hübner, J.F., Wooldridge, M.: Programming Multi-agent Systems in AgentSpeak Using Jason, vol. 8. Wiley, Hoboken (2007)
3. Rao, A.S.: AgentSpeak(L): BDI agents speak out in a logical computable language. In: Van de Velde, W., Perram, J.W. (eds.) MAAMAW 1996. LNCS, vol. 1038, pp. 42–55. Springer, Heidelberg (1996). https://doi.org/10.1007/BFb0031845
4. Rao, A.S., Georgeff, M.P.: Modeling rational agents within a BDI-architecture. In: Proceedings of the 2nd International Conference on Principles of Knowledge Representation and Reasoning, pp. 473–484 (1991)
5. Winikoff, M., Padgham, L., Harland, J., Thangarajah, J.: Declarative and procedural goals in intelligent agent systems. In: Proceedings of KR 2002, pp. 470–481 (2002)
6. Dastani, M.: 2APL: a practical agent programming language. Int. J. Auton. Agents Multi-Agent Syst. (JAAMAS) **16**(3), 214–248 (2008). Special Issue on Computational Logic-based Agents, Toni, F., Bentahar, J. (eds.)

7. Boissier, O., Bordini, R.H., Hübner, J.F., Ricci, A., Santi, A.: Multi-agent oriented programming with JaCaMo. Sci. Comput. Program. **78**, 747–761 (2013)
8. Brooks, R.: A robust layered control system for a mobile robot. IEEE J. Robot. Autom. **2**(1), 14–23 (1986). https://doi.org/10.1109/JRA.1986.1087032
9. Bratman, M.E., Israel, D.J., Pollack, M.E.: Plans and resource-bounded practical reasoning. Comput. Intell. **4**, 349–355 (1988)
10. MAPC 2019. https://multiagentcontest.org/2019/. Accessed 14 May 2020

GOAL-DTU: Development of Distributed Intelligence for the Multi-Agent Programming Contest

Alexander Birch Jensen and Jørgen Villadsen[✉]

Algorithms, Logic and Graphs Section, Department of Applied Mathematics and Computer Science, Technical University of Denmark, Richard Petersens Plads, Building 324, 2800 Kongens Lyngby, Denmark
jovi@dtu.dk

Abstract. We provide a brief description of the GOAL-DTU system for the Multi-Agent Programming Contest, including the overall strategy and how the system is designed to apply this strategy. Our agents are implemented using the GOAL programming language. We evaluate the performance of our agents for the contest, and finally also discuss how to improve the system based on analysis of its strengths and weaknesses.

1 Introduction

In fall 2019 we participated as the GOAL-DTU team in the annual Multi-Agent Programming Contest (MAPC). We are using the GOAL agent programming language [1–3] and we are affiliated with the Technical University of Denmark (DTU). We participated in the contest in 2009 and 2010 as the Jason-DTU team [4,5], in 2011 and 2012 as the Python-DTU team [6,7], in 2013 and 2014 as the GOAL-DTU team [8], in 2015/2016 as the Python-DTU team [9] and in 2017 and 2018 as the Jason-DTU team [10].

In 2019 we had the new *Agents Assemble* scenario. The paper is organized as follows:

- Section 2 describes agent programming using the GOAL language.
- Section 3 covers the overall strategy of our agents.
- Section 4 describes the knowledge our agents acquire from the environment.
- Section 5 describes how our agents communicate.
- Section 6 describes the movement of our agents.
- Section 7 covers how our agents complete selected tasks.
- Section 8 evaluates the performance of our agents in the three matchups.
- Section 9 discusses improvements to the system.
- Section 10 is our conclusion.

T. Ahlbrecht et al. (Eds.): MAPC 2019, LNAI 12381, pp. 79–105, 2020.
https://doi.org/10.1007/978-3-030-59299-8_4

2   Agent Programming in GOAL

This section introduces the basic concepts of the GOAL agent programming language that are relevant to the implementation of our system.

Agents in GOAL are to be understood as self-controlled independent entities. Each agent interacts with the environment and communicates with other agents. Percepts and messages are treated as events that can be processed. This event processing then feeds into the knowledge, beliefs and goals (the three components that comprise an agent's cognitive state).

The programming philosophy behind GOAL is quite different when compared to other popular agent programming languages. Beyond the cognitive state, the core abilities of an agent are the just mentioned event processing capability, the ability to represent knowledge and reason about it, and finally, rule-based decision-making which allows an agent to select an action based on its current cognitive state.

2.1   The GOAL Execution Loop

GOAL features a simple execution loop of each agent. Beyond an initialization module that can process the initial state of the environment, and set up the initial cognitive state, GOAL follows the execution loop below:

1. **Check new events:** If there are no new events, the next step is skipped.
2. **Process events:** The event module processes new events. Recall that these events are either percepts from the environment or messages from other agents. It is the purpose of this module to update the cognitive state of the agent before selecting the next action.
3. **Action selection:** The main module defines the rules for decision-making. Based on the rules, the first valid action is selected. Note that several actions may be applicable based on the rules in the main module. GOAL allows for other strategies, but it is essential to our implementation that the first action is always the one that is selected.
4. **Perform action:** The selected action is sent to the environment (and communication actions are executed internally).

Technically speaking, there is also a final step that applies the post-conditions (effects) for the selected action from our action specification. However, it is not relevant for us since we rely solely on the event module to perceive the effects of actions.

2.2   Action Selection

GOAL advocates that agents are individual entities that reason about their environment. They react to changes in their environment rather than executing predetermined plans. For example, an agent may devise a plan for a goal to be achieved. At some intermediate step in the plan, the next step may no longer be applicable due to (unforeseen) changes in the environment. GOAL tries to avoid the complexity of rebuilding "broken plans" by advocating a reactive model. We should consider how the agent can select appropriate actions based on the current state of affairs. However, note that it is still possible for programmers to represent plans via the cognitive state of agents using Prolog, but it is not facilitated explicitly by the language. The reactive approach is not flawless either: it can be difficult for programmers to come up with logical rules that produce the desired behaviour, but by overcoming this challenge, we often have a more flexible agent.

3 Strategy

In our current system, we have a universal agent type. By a universal agent type we mean that all agents share the same logic. While it is possible to have different kinds of agents in GOAL, i.e. via modules, it is not something we currently utilize. Some advantages of a universal agent type are that it is faster to implement, every agent is seamlessly capable of everything and we need not worry about when to switch the agent's type. The main disadvantage is that the code base becomes convoluted as development progresses due to growing array of logical rules for selecting the appropriate action.

During action selection, the agents apply heuristic measures to determine movement directions. We describe the different variants of heuristic functions in Sect. 6. It should also be noted that we currently do not perform any *clear* actions. We did not manage to implement use of the action in a meaningful way for the contest.

The following priority list describes the decision-making process of our agents (with some simplifications) where the first applicable rule determines the action to be selected in a given state:

- If the agent is assigned to a task:
  - Detach any attached blocks not needed for the task. The agent will only detach blocks if it considers it non-obstructive to future movement. If not, it will continue to move (using the detach movement heuristic) until it considers it safe to detach.
  - Rotate the block into the position dictated by the task plan. If rotation is blocked, move until rotation is possible (using the exploration movement heuristic).
  - If the agent observes part of the pattern to be handed in, or if the agent is assigned to submit the task (the submitting agent), and is on a goal, wait for other agents (by performing the *skip* action).
  - If the agent observes the entire pattern, connect with other blocks/agents as described by the task plan.
  - If all blocks in the pattern are connected, the assigned agent submits the task.
  - If the agent finds the submitting agent (waiting in a goal area), move until the attachment(s) form the (partial) pattern (using the task pattern movement heuristic).

- If the agent is the submitting agent, move towards a goal area (using the go to movement heuristics).
- Else, move towards the position of the submitting agent (using the go to movement heuristics).
- If a goal area is known, move towards it (using the go to movement heuristics).
- Move into the most promising direction (based on the exploration movement heuristic).
– If the agent is not assigned to a task:
  - If a block or dispenser is in vision, and the agent does not have four blocks:
    * Rotate such that a free attachment spot is facing the direction of the block/dispenser. If rotation is blocked, move (using the exploration movement heuristic).
    * If the agent is next to a block, attach it to the agent.
    * If the agent is next to a dispenser, request a block.
    * If not next to the block/dispenser, move towards it (using the go to movement heuristics).
  - Move around on the map (based on the safe exploration heuristic).
– Perform *skip* action.

4   Agent Knowledge

In this section, we cover the design of the knowledge stored in the agents' mental states. Generally speaking, the agents store and maintain knowledge about the map that is assumed be invariable (or alternatively: always perceivable). We consider invariable knowledge to be: the positions of goal cells, attached blocks, the agent's current position (relative to its starting position), positions visited by the agent, and the position of encountered agents from the team. Some of these involve communication between agents. The positions of blocks, dispensers and obstacles are only stored in the agent as long as they are within vision. The communication of our agents is described in Sect. 5.

The agent does not perceive a global view of the map via the environment, nor its own position on the map. Furthermore, random events and actions of other agents can change the structure of the map over time. Due to this complexity, we do not attempt to build up an internal representation of the map. Unfortunately, this comes at the cost of efficient and meaningful movement on the map.

4.1   The Current Position

By keeping track of performed *move* actions, and checking for a potential failed action, the agent maintains information about its own current position. With the starting position of the agent as the center of origin, we maintain two values that represent the agent's position in a two-dimensional space. Moving in a direction, either north, east, south or west; results in incrementing or decrementing one of these values.

4.2   Visited Positions

The bookkeeping of visited positions is essential to avoiding that the agent repeatedly gets stuck, or does not make progress. When an agent performs a *move* action, in the next step the following information about the visited position is stored: the relative position of the agent, the current step in the simulation, and a flag for if the position is a goal cell. The position is stored relative to the initial position of each agent. That is, each agent is initially at $(x, y) = (0, 0)$. The relative position of each agent is updated based on successful *move* actions.

As the simulation progresses, the database of visited positions gains additional entries. Due to the way we utilize this, we are only interested in visited positions with respect to a specific subtasks. For instance, if the agent is trying to find a goal cell, it is not relevant which positions the agent visited in an attempt to find blocks. Therefore, we define a number of events that trigger a clearing of the agent's knowledge about visited positions:

- The agent has completed a subtask: Attached, detached or requested a block.
- We submitted a task. In our system, once a task is submitted, most agents will work on different matters.

The visited nodes are useful for steering the agent away from repeating the same movement patterns when they do not make progress. The idea is that visited positions are only relevant locally – at later points in time it may be relevant to visit those positions again. Essentially, this means that the visited positions are only remembered for the duration of smaller subtasks. Intuitively, it seems non-optimal to remove knowledge that could help steer the agent away from dead ends that it has found earlier. However, the ever-changing structure of the map quickly invalidates this knowledge anyway.

4.3   Positions of Goal Cells

The positions of goal cells are assumed to be invariable throughout the simulation. Due to this assumption, once the agents store knowledge about the positions of goal cells, they are never removed.

The position of goal cells are stored relative to the position of the agents and are thus updated following successful *move* actions.

The agents learn about positions of goal cells either through perceiving them within their own vision or via communication with other agents.

4.4   Blocks, Dispensers and Obstacles

The information about blocks, dispensers and obstacles are only perceived when the agent is within vision. A *clear* event may remove blocks from the map, or they may be moved by other agents. Due to this, the positions of blocks is not maintained when outside of the agent's vision.

Obstacle positions could potentially be maintained by perceiving *clear* events and remove information about affected obstacles. The position of obstacles currently plays no part in any sort of route finding algorithm and we do not maintain this knowledge when outside of the agent's vision.

Dispensers are different from blocks and obstacles as their positions do not change during the simulation. In the current implementation, agents always go towards an available dispenser, if they do not have a block on each side, and if they are not trying to solve a task. Our agents will always prefer to go to the nearest known position of a block or dispenser. Thus to avoid the agent always going back to the same dispenser, we currently do not keep information of dispenser positions outside of the agent's vision.

Neither the position of blocks, dispenser or obstacles are shared between agents via communication. Since we do not keep and maintain their positions, it does not make sense to share the information between agents – it should only be part of an agent's mental state when within vision.

4.5   Attached Blocks

Each agent keeps track of its own attached blocks with coordinates relative to its own position. The environment makes available any attached blocks in vision, but it is not immediately visible which agents the blocks are attached to. To make sure that the agent only keeps stored knowledge about the blocks attached to itself, we check for successful *attach* actions to insert the knowledge of a block being attached. Successful rotations update the stored coordinates accordingly. We always make sure that any knowledge about attached blocks is also perceivable in the environment – if not, the knowledge is removed. This is due to the fact that submitting tasks and *clear* events may invalidate the knowledge.

We will also briefly mention that current attached blocks are communicated between agents. This is used for devising plans to submit tasks. The details are covered in Sects. 5.3 and 7.2.

5   Agent Communication and Shared Knowledge

Sharing knowledge between agents by means of communication is essential for efficiently exploiting the multiple agents available. The environment presents a number of challenges in enabling effective agent communication. Also, the volatility of the scenario map does not suggest an easy way of building up a shared representation. Our current implementation could utilize more shared knowledge and communication, and it is something we hope to improve in the future.

Specifically for agent programming using GOAL, communication between agents are part of the core loop. One important aspect is that any messages sent in one step will only be available for processing by the receiving agent in the following step. This requires some deliberate implementation to make sure that the information received is up to date – in our implementation this is extremely relevant as we often share information that is relative to the current position of agents.

5.1   Encountering Other Agents

The environment only gives information to agents about the position of other agents when within their vision. The agent is able to perceive which team an encountered agent belongs to, but no further identification is provided (i.e. the name of the encountered agent). To be able to identify which pair of agents that have encountered each other we apply the following: when two of our agents meet, they exchange information about what other objects they are able to identify within their vision. Only if they agree on everything in their shared vision, they acknowledge that they did in fact encounter each other. A check is performed to prevent two agents from mistakenly concluding that they encountered each other. We do this by checking that the given pair of agents agree on objects in their shared vision. Our initial implementation was solely based on the agents' relative position to each other, with no additional conditions, which yielded occasional false positives.

5.2   Goal Cells and Agent Positions

When two agents agree that they encountered each other, they exchange information about the positions of goal cells and other agents from the team. Each agent adds the shared information to its belief base relative to its belief about its own current position. Currently, the agents do not continue to share new information after encountering other agents.

When an agent successfully moves in a given direction, it informs other agents about which directed it moved in. This information is used by each agent to maintain the knowledge about positions of other agents.

5.3   Attached Blocks

We assign one of our agents as the *planning agent*. At each step of the simulation, each agent, that is not currently assigned to solve a task, sends a message to the planning agent containing a list of its currently attached blocks. The planning agent uses the received messages to (possibly) assign a task to a subset of the agents that sent messages. The details of the task planning assignment are covered in Sect. 7.2.

6   Agent Movement

The *Agents Assemble* scenario provides only partial vision of the map to agents, limited to a small area around each agent. Combining the knowledge of agents over time will provide more and more knowledge of the map. However, random *clear* events happen over time around the map that remove and randomly add new obstacles on part of the map. Other agents also have the ability to remove obstacles. As such, a usual route finding algorithm requires substantial alterations to be usable for the scenario. Due to the volatility of the map, such a route finding algorithm will necessarily have to support re-planning when the planned route is invalidated.

The above mentioned challenges for a route finding algorithm means that we have opted for a more naive implementation of agent movement. The overall strategy is to evaluate each of the (up to four) possible directions: north, east, south and west; and then select the direction which has the optimal heuristic value. When multiple directions share the same optimal value, a direction is selected pseudo-randomly (the current simulation step is used as seed). Our agent movement algorithm has five different variations:

- **Exploration** favors directions towards positions the agent has not visited recently.
- **Safe exploration** is similar to the above, but further favors directions that increase the distance to goal areas and other agents.
- **Go to** favors directions towards a given relative position and penalizes movement to recently visited positions on the map.
- **Task pattern** favors directions that realize a given task pattern and penalizes movement to recently visited positions on the map.
- **Detach** favors directions away from obstacles.

The choice of movement algorithm depends on the current strategy of the agent.

6.1 Evaluation Functions

As described above, each variation of the movement algorithm is distinguished by its heuristic function h. We will use h^+ to denote that a higher value is better and h^- when lower is better. Neither of the mathematical formulations are perfect in any sense, but give some approximation of the optimal choice.

Exploration

$$h_{exp}^+(d) = \sum_{visited} \begin{cases} \frac{|\Delta x(d)| + |\Delta y(d)|}{\Delta S^2} & \text{if } |\Delta x(d)| + |\Delta y(d)| \leq 30 \text{ and } \Delta S > 0 \\ 0 & \text{else} \end{cases}$$

where $\Delta x(d)$ and $\Delta y(d)$ are the differences in x and y coordinates between the visited position and the agent's position after performing *move* in direction d. ΔS is the number of steps since the position was visited.

Safe Exploration

$$h_{s-exp}^+(d) = h_{exp}^+(d) + \sum_{(x_t, y_t) \in P} c(x_t, y_t) * (|x_t| + |y_t|)$$

where P is a set of coordinates of goal cells and nearby agents in the team. x_t and y_t are coordinates relative to the agent's current position. $c(x_t, y_t)$ is a constant factor used for heavily favoring moving away from nearby agents.

Go To

$$h_{go-to}^{-}(d) = |\Delta x(d)| + |\Delta y(d)| + \text{size}(V_{p_d})$$

where $\Delta x(d)$ and $\Delta y(d)$ are the differences in x and y coordinates between the goal position and p_d is the agent's position after performing *move* in direction d. $\text{size}(V_{p_d})$ is the number of times position p_d has been visited recently.

Task Pattern

$$h_{pat}^{-}(d) = \text{size}(V_{p_d}) + \sum_{(x,y,t) \in (pat/att)} min\left\{|\Delta x| + |\Delta y|, |\Psi(d, x, y, t, \Delta x, \Delta y)|\right\}$$

where $\text{size}(V_{p_d})$ is the number of times p_d has been visited recently (p_d is the agent's position after performing *move* in direction d). The set pat/att contains the relative position and type of every block in the pattern excluding the blocks the agent itself is providing (has attached). The predicate $\Psi(d, x, y, t, \Delta x, \Delta y)$ gives the difference in x and y coordinates to every observed non-attached block of type t assuming a move in direction d.

Detach

$$h_{det}^{+}(d) = h_{exp}^{+}(d) + \sum_{(x,y) \in \text{obstacles}} |\Delta x(d)| + |\Delta y(d)|$$

where obstacles is the set of the positions of observable obstacles. $|\Delta x(d)|$ and $|\Delta y(d)|$ are the relative differences in x and y coordinates between the agent and the obstacle following a move in direction d.

7   Solving Tasks

This section describes how the agents solve tasks. We consider solving a task to consist of four parts: Collecting blocks, planning tasks to complete based on the collected blocks, executing task plans (assembling the pattern) and finally submitting the pattern.

7.1   Collecting Blocks

One core aspect of our strategy is to collect blocks before committing to any of the available tasks, and to only commit to tasks for which we already have the blocks to solve.

If an agent, that is not assigned to a task, and does not hold a block on each side, encounters a block or dispenser, it will generally try to go towards it. It will only ignore the possibility to collect the block(s) in case another from the same team is adjacent to it. This is to avoid race conditions for the same resource and improve efficiency. Dealing with this issue via communication would likely be a better approach, however.

In case the agent sees a dispenser or block, that is not occupied by another agent from the same team, the agent will rotate if necessary to ensure that a free attachment spot is available in the direction of the block or dispenser. Attaching blocks takes priority over requesting blocks from dispensers. The agent will repeatedly attach blocks on each of the four spots until they are all used.

In some cases the position of the block or dispenser may not allow the agent to attach from that angle due to its current attachments. This is not currently checked and avoided. In such a case, the agent is likely to enter a state of not making progress – unless it is assigned to a task, or if it moves outside of vision of the block due to being penalized for going to similar positions repeatedly.

7.2 Task Planning

If the combined attachments of all agents are sufficient to solve a task the planning agent will compute a task plan for it. The task with the lowest reward (and thus, likely the easiest to complete) is selected. We select the easiest task based on the observed performance of the agents, and we only ever try to complete one task at a time. The logic for task planning supports computing multiple non-overlapping task plans, but we observed that the agents would be likely to obstruct each other. We only ever commit to a task that has some amount of steps available to complete the task before the deadline. For the contest, we set this to a minimum of 50 steps to complete the task. Later experimentation has yielded better results with a higher number. Due to the abundance of available tasks, the improved results seem logical. So far we have not conducted tests of the distribution of task completion times for our agents.

The task plan specifies how each agent provides part of the pattern including how it should be rotated. The expected completed pattern is computed for each agent relative to its own position in the aligned pattern. This is used to ensure that the agents align their attachments correctly. The task plan also specifies how agents should connect to each other once the pattern alignment step is complete. For each task, one of the selected agents is assigned to submit the task.

The task plans are rigid in the sense that two agents that provide the same block type cannot swap their respective sub-patterns. While there potentially could be some benefit in supporting this behaviour, we do not consider it worth the effort to implement when considering other potential improvements to the agents.

7.3 Executing Task Plans

When a task plan is sent to the agents, the agents not involved will keep on moving around the map, but their heuristics for movement will penalize moving close to other agents. This is done in an attempt to avoid obstructing agents that are working on completing a task. Each of the involved agents will immediately detach any of the blocks that are no longer needed and rotate the remaining attachments to align with their part of the pattern for the task. The agent responsible for submitting the task will move towards the nearest goal cell if its position is known (or scout for a goal cell if not). Once positioned at a goal cell, the agent will wait for the other agents to show up. If the other agents assigned to the task know the position of the agent responsible to submitting the task, they will move towards that agent. If not, they will methodically visit each of the known goal areas. If this fails, they will scout around the map. In most practical cases, the agents eventually learn of the position of the agent responsible for submitting the task.

We are not currently able to resolve situations where assigned agents are stuck. However, the task plan is discarded if an assigned agent is disabled due to a *clear* event. The idea is that if an agent is stuck the task plan is to be discarded, but our implementation does not work properly. As previously mentioned, we also do not utilize the *clear* action in any way currently, which could solve potential pathing problems. At any time, if the task deadline is exceeded, the task plan is deleted.

In case an agent assigned to the task finds its way to the agent responsible for submitting the task, waiting at a goal area, the agent will start to align itself to complete the pattern. This is achieved by the task pattern heuristic that favors directions that minimize the expected deviance from the pattern to submit. It should be noted that the agent responsible for submitting the task will try to position itself such that the other agents have room to align themselves to complete the pattern.

Once the pattern is complete, the agents connect their attachments and the task is submitted.

8   Evaluation of Matches

With a total of four participants, we played three matches against each of the three opponents. In the following, we evaluate the performance of our agents in each matchup. See Figs. 1–45 for key statistics over the 500 steps of each match.

GOAL-DTU vs. TRG

In two of the simulations, we manage to complete a single task early on (Figs. 10, 11, 12). Team TRG completes a single task in the first simulation, but are unable to do so in the other simulations. TRG has a strategy where some of their agents defend goal areas by attempting to perform *clear* actions on our agents trying to complete tasks. Since part of our task execution plan is to assemble the pattern in the goal area, the strategy of team TRG denies a fair number of submits from our agents.

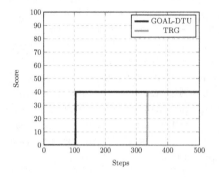

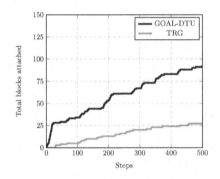

Fig. 1. Score: GOAL-DTU vs. TRG (1)   **Fig. 2.** Score: GOAL-DTU vs. TRG (2)

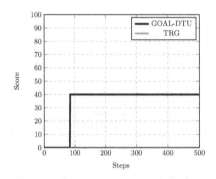

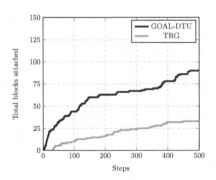

Fig. 3. Score: GOAL-DTU vs. TRG (3)   **Fig. 4.** Blocks: GOAL-DTU vs. TRG (1)

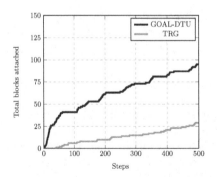

Fig. 5. Blocks: GOAL-DTU vs. TRG (2)   **Fig. 6.** Blocks: GOAL-DTU vs. TRG (3)

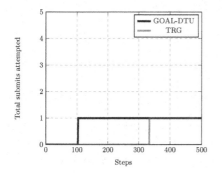

Fig. 7. Submit: GOAL-DTU vs. TRG (1)

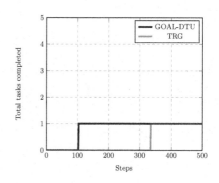

Fig. 8. Submit: GOAL-DTU vs. TRG (2)

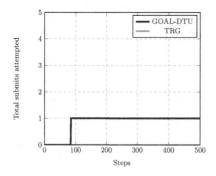

Fig. 9. Submit: GOAL-DTU vs. TRG (3)

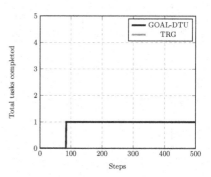

Fig. 10. Tasks: GOAL-DTU vs. TRG (1)

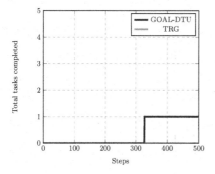

Fig. 11. Tasks: GOAL-DTU vs. TRG (2)

Fig. 12. Tasks: GOAL-DTU vs. TRG (3)

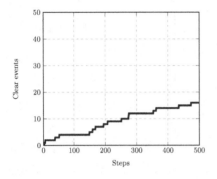

Fig. 13. Clear: GOAL-DTU vs. TRG (1)

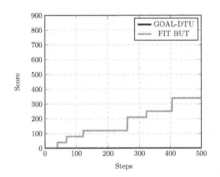

Fig. 14. Clear: GOAL-DTU vs. TRG (2)

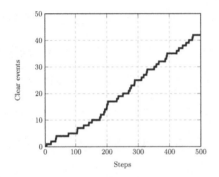

Fig. 15. Clear: GOAL-DTU vs. TRG (3)

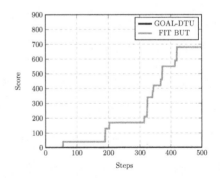

Fig. 16. Score: GOAL-DTU vs. FIT BUT (1)

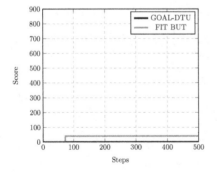

Fig. 17. Score: GOAL-DTU vs. FIT BUT (2)

Fig. 18. Score: GOAL-DTU vs. FIT BUT (3)

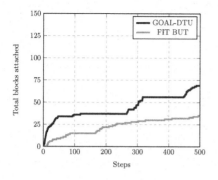

Fig. 19. Blocks: GOAL-DTU vs. FIT BUT (1)

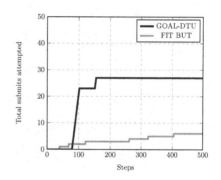

Fig. 20. Blocks: GOAL-DTU vs. FIT BUT (2)

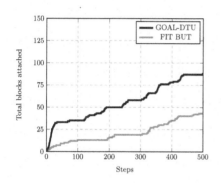

Fig. 21. Blocks: GOAL-DTU vs. FIT BUT (3)

Fig. 22. Submit: GOAL-DTU vs. FIT BUT (1)

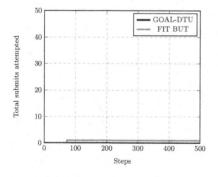

Fig. 23. Submit: GOAL-DTU vs. FIT BUT (2)

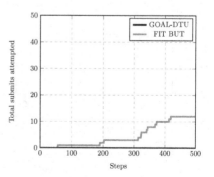

Fig. 24. Submit: GOAL-DTU vs. FIT BUT (3)

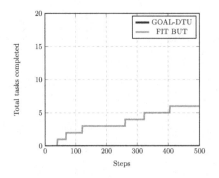

Fig. 25. Tasks: GOAL-DTU vs. FIT BUT (1)

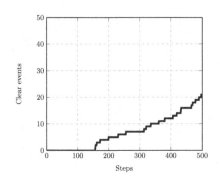

Fig. 26. Tasks: GOAL-DTU vs. FIT BUT (2)

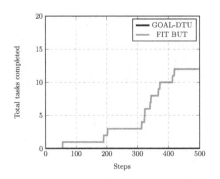

Fig. 27. Tasks: GOAL-DTU vs. FIT BUT (3)

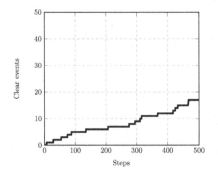

Fig. 29. Clear: GOAL-DTU vs. FIT BUT (2)

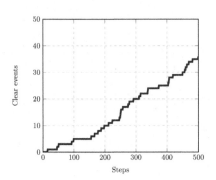

Fig. 28. Clear: GOAL-DTU vs. FIT BUT (1)

Fig. 30. Clear: GOAL-DTU vs. FIT BUT (3)

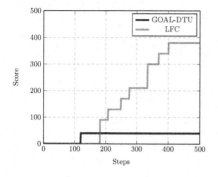

Fig. 31. Score: GOAL-DTU vs. LFC (1)

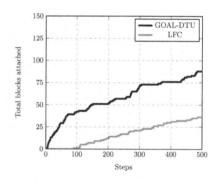

Fig. 32. Score: GOAL-DTU vs. LFC (2)

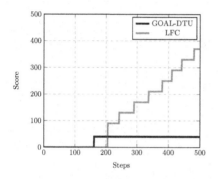

Fig. 33. Score: GOAL-DTU vs. LFC (3)

Fig. 34. Blocks: GOAL-DTU vs. LFC (1)

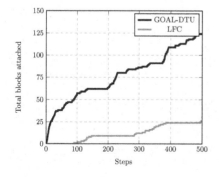

Fig. 35. Blocks: GOAL-DTU vs. LFC (2)

Fig. 36. Blocks: GOAL-DTU vs. LFC (3)

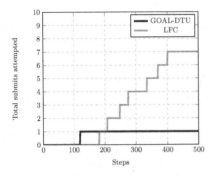

Fig. 37. Submit: GOAL-DTU vs. LFC (1)

Fig. 38. Submit: GOAL-DTU vs. LFC (2)

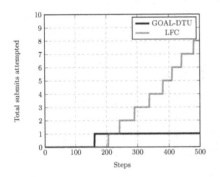

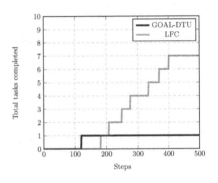

Fig. 39. Submit: GOAL-DTU vs. LFC (3)

Fig. 40. Tasks: GOAL-DTU vs. LFC (1)

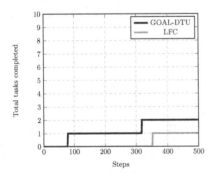

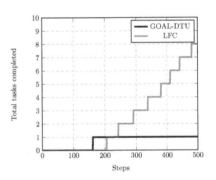

Fig. 41. Tasks: GOAL-DTU vs. LFC (2)

Fig. 42. Tasks: GOAL-DTU vs. LFC (3)

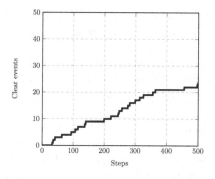
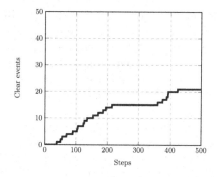

Fig. 43. Clear: GOAL-DTU vs. LFC (1)   **Fig. 44.** Clear: GOAL-DTU vs. LFC (2)

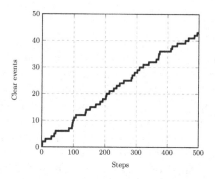

Fig. 45. Clear: GOAL-DTU vs. LFC (3)

We experience problems with many agent getting stuck in every simulation. Around halfway through, we can usually observe that half of our agents are now stuck. This is especially detrimental if one of those agents is assigned to complete a task.

It seems that our greedy approach for collecting blocks, which causes the map to become even more convoluted, also causes serious issues for the agents of team TRG.

In the third simulation, the number of blocks we manage to collect stagnates (Fig. 6). This could be correlated with the number of *clear* events that is significantly higher (Fig. 15). While this presumably has no direct impact our score, it could be an indication towards our agents' ability to move around on the map.

See Figs. 1–15 for all of the collected statistics in matches vs. TRG.

GOAL-DTU vs. FIT BUT

For this matchup we experienced issues with the agents. In the first simulation, our agents manage to assemble two patterns for tasks, but in one instance they seem to have a wrong pattern, and in the other instance they try to submit outside of a goal area (Fig. 22). At this point, we try to restart our agents, but they do not mange to make meaningful progress since our implementation is not robust in case of crashes (Fig. 19).

Also in the second simulation we have to attempt a restart, but to no avail. It seems our agents obstruct the map so severely that team FIT BUT has issues (Fig. 26). Before our agents crash, they are relatively close to assembling a pattern.

The story repeats itself in the third simulation, although team FIT BUT successfully complete multiple tasks (Fig. 27).

While we do not expect us to have been able to beat the agents of team FIT BUT, we would likely have been able to complete a few tasks if the agents did not crash.

See Figs. 16–30 for all of the collected statistics in matches vs. FIT BUT.

LFC vs. GOAL-DTU

We managed to complete tasks in each of the three simulations (Figs. 40, 41, 42). Yet, as for other simulations, as the simulation progresses, the agents' ability to move around the map degrades (Figs. 34, 35, 36). In comparison, it seems that the agents of team LFC make steady progress throughout the simulation (Figs. 40, 41, 42). Another note about the agents of team LFC is there seems to be a correlation between the tasks they submit and the number of blocks they collect which suggest a different strategy (Figs. 34, 35, 36).

We manage to complete more tasks in the second simulation (Fig. 41). By inspection of the map layout, there are two goal areas in the middle of map, not close to any obstacles. This is a lucky coincidence for our agents, as they often experience more problems when close to obstacles (maneuverability in confined spaces is more likely to degrade over time).

See Figs. 31–45 for all of the collected statistics in matches vs. LFC.

9   Discussion

While our implementation achieved satisfying results, it can still be improved on several fronts. During the contest, we learned that the performance of the agents could be improved by tinkering with parameters, while other issues were due to technical difficulties.

9.1   Changes Since the Contest

After analysis of the replays of our matches in the contest, we realized two possible improvements to the implementation. The first improvement is concerned with the assumed time our agents need to complete a task. Through experimentation, we have learned that increasing the minimum amount of steps needed to complete a task improved the performance of the agents significantly. The value used for the matches in the contest often lead to agents missing task deadlines resulting in a lower score, when considering that a task with a later deadline could have been chosen instead.

Another issue occurs when agents detach blocks (for getting rid of blocks not needed for completing the assigned task). The agents will try to detach the unneeded blocks away from goal areas and obstacles. This is done to avoid that the agent potentially obstructs itself and other agents. By increasing the minimum distance there should be to goal cells and obstacles when detaching a block, we observed improved performance.

9.2   Technical Issues During the Contest

During the contest, we experienced a number of issues during the simulations that we had not encountered before. Unfortunately, for some of the matches this made our agents break down completely, practically leaving us with no way to continue. Since we did not experience this before, our agents are not very robust in the sense that they are not well-suited for restarts during the simulation in case of crashes.

One of the issues we experienced occurs when the steps are performed very rapidly, at which point it seems as if the GOAL execution and the server get out of sync. We did not experience this problem earlier since in our testing, there were always agents not performing actions, thus using the full server timeout for each step. Experimentation following the contest shows that the problem is not related to connection issues and will have to be investigated further. We find that two seconds for each step prevents the issue.

9.3   Known Problems and Bugs

In our implementation, we have discovered a number of problems over time, and there are still some unresolved bugs to fix.

One problem is related to agents getting stuck. Often in simulations, we will experience that one or more of our agents end up getting stuck. This could be due to a number of random *clear* events, or potentially the map has disconnected parts. One of the major issues with this is that we have not been able to implement a way for agents to deduce that they are in fact stuck, or that some agents are unable to reach each other. Another problem is that we do not utilize the *clear* action to help the agents become unstuck.

Lastly, we have experienced problems when agents assigned to a task visit goal areas in search for the agent responsible for submitting the task. Due to an unresolved bug, the agents will not properly scout all the goal areas, but tend to always stay in the same area. This obviously means that we will never be able to submit unless the problematic agents learn about the position of the agent responsible for submitting the task.

9.4   Improvements

There are a number of directions to take in terms of improving the implementation. We will consider some of our high-level ideas to improve the performance of the system by targeting some of our weaknesses.

Our agents are universal in the sense that every agent is based on exactly the same logic rules. One way to improve the performance, could be to assign different roles to agents, or to assign agents into smaller teams that move together. Examples of roles could be agents that explore the map, some that request and collect blocks and some that complete tasks using the collected blocks.

Another weakness of our agents is poor movement. Since we do not build an internal representation of the map during the simulation, our agents often move blindly. We expect substantially improved performance if we are able to make the agents better at moving around the map, for example by building up such an internal map representation (which could then be shared among agents). The initial reason not to attempt building up a map representation, is the complexity of the map being dynamic.

Another problem arises from our greedy approach to collecting blocks. Since each agent always tries to collect one block on each side, movement around the map becomes much harder afterwards. Furthermore, we do not consider the possibility that an agent may be able to move past narrow corridors by rotating its attachments, or potentially even moving the blocks past corridors a few at a time.

The last obvious improvement is to implement some logic to perform *clear* actions. Multiple *clear* events are likely to make it difficult to move around the map. Getting rid of obstructions is exactly one of the purposes of the *clear* action. It can be used to reconnect parts of the map that has been disconnected completely, and to save valuable time by creating shortcuts through obstacles.

Lastly, there are number of technical improvements that we would like to implement. Since it was impossible to monitor the agents live during the simulations of the contest, it would have been helpful to have better output (in the console) about the behaviour and progress of the agents. Furthermore, we would like to increase the robustness of the agents in case of crashes such that they can be restarted and still make progress.

10   Conclusion

We have provided an overview of the multi-agent system that the GOAL-DTU team developed for the Multi-Agent Programming Contest 2019. We have explained our choice of the GOAL programming language; we have also described the main strategy of our agents and how they execute that strategy. This year was the first iteration using the *Agents Assemble* scenario, and we have developed our implementation from scratch using GOAL. Our implementation features a universal agent type in which each agent is based on the same set of logical rules.

The strengths of our system are the flexible nature of our agents. Our agents always react to the current state of affairs and do not rely heavily on predefined plans to reach their goal of completing tasks. The weaknesses are primarily the agents' poor movement around the map and rigidity in the way tasks are assigned and submitted where stuck agents have a severe negative impact on the performance of the system.

Finally, we have described how to improve the system by coming up with ideas that target its weaknesses. Some of these potential improvements are related to minor issues and bug fixes while other potential improvements require designing and refactoring large parts of the system.

In conclusion, we are satisfied with the performance of our system, ending at a 3rd place in the final rankings, when considering that we have built the system from scratch. We consider our current implementation a good platform to built on for future iterations of the *Agents Assemble* scenario.

Further details about the previous DTU teams are available here: https://people.compute.dtu.dk/jovi/MAS/

Acknowledgement. We thank Tobias Ahlbrecht, Asta Halkjær From, Benjamin Simon Stenbjerg Jepsen, John Bruntse Larsen and Simon Rumle Tarnow for discussions.

A   Team Overview: Short Answers

A.1   Participants and Their Background

- **What was your motivation to participate in the contest?** To work on implementing a multi-agent system capable of competing in a realistic, albeit simulated, scenario.
- **What is the history of your group? (course project, thesis, ...)**
  The name of our team is GOAL-DTU. We participated in the contest in 2009 and 2010 as the Jason-DTU team [4,5], in 2011 and 2012 as the Python-DTU team [6,7], in 2013 and 2014 as the GOAL-DTU team [8], in 2015/2016 as the Python-DTU team [9] and in 2017 and 2018 as the Jason-DTU team [10]. The members of the team are as follows:
    - Jørgen Villadsen, PhD
    - Alexander Birch Jensen, PhD student
  Asta Halkjær From, MSc student and now PhD student, was a consultant until the tournament started.
  We are affiliated with the Algorithms, Logic and Graphs section at DTU Compute, Department of Applied Mathematics and Computer Science, Technical University of Denmark (DTU). DTU Compute is located in the greater Copenhagen area. The main contact is associate professor Jørgen Villadsen, email: jovi@dtu.dk
- **What is your field of research? Which work therein is related?** We are responsible for the Artificial Intelligence and Algorithms study line of the MSc in Computer Science and Engineering programme.

A.2   Statistics

How much time did you invest in the contest (for programming, organizing your group, other)? Approximately 200 man hours

How many lines of code did you produce for your final agent team? Approximately 1000 lines

How many people were involved? 3 (1 programming)

When did you start working on your agents? August 2019

A.3   Agent system details

How does the team work together? (i.e. coordination, information sharing, ...) How decentralised is your approach? A task is delegated to a set of agents that are attached to the needed blocks. One agent is assigned as the so-called submit agent and the other agents follow/search for this submit agent before aligning the pattern in a goal area. Beyond this, each agent keeps track of the position of other agents. This information is exchanged when two agents are within vision range. The agents confirm their identify by agreeing on the part of the environment they both are able to perceive based on vision.

Do your agents make use of the following features: Planning, Learning, Organisations, Norms? If so, please elaborate briefly. Planning is used when delegating tasks. Agents have set positions in the final pattern for submission.

Can your agents change their behavior during runtime? If so, what triggers the changes? The agent's behavior changes if they are delegated a submission task. Furthermore, other agents will try to avoid blocking agents with a task.

Did you have to make changes to the team (e.g. fix critical bugs) during the contest? We encountered timeout problems when the simulations ran too fast. We did not manage to resolve this beyond putting artificial limit. Furthermore, we did not manage to handle the automatic transition between simulations in each matchup.

How did you go about debugging your system? Partly using the debugger and partly using console output.

During the contest you were not allowed to watch the matches. How did you understand what your team of agents was doing? Did this understanding help you to improve your team's performance? We tracked them using console output although this feature could be vastly improved. It did not help towards performance beyond discovering timeout problems in fast simulations.

Did you invest time in making your agents more robust? How? Some robustness comes almost for free using GOAL as we never deeply commit to a plan. We also considered tracking if an agent ending being stuck, but ultimately the feature was not completed.

A.4   Scenario and Strategy

What is the main strategy of your agent team?
- If the agent is selected to hand in blocks for a task (part of a task plan):
  - Detach any attached blocks not needed for the task. The agent will only detach blocks if it considers it non-obstructive to future movement. If not, it will move until it reaches a position where it considers it safe to detach.
  - Rotate the block into the position dictated by the task plan. If rotation is blocked, move until rotation is possible.
  - If the agent observes part of the pattern to be handed in, or if the agent is the one to submit the task and is on a goal, wait for other agents (skip action).
  - If the agent observes the entire pattern, connect with other agents as described by the task plan and then submit (the *submit* action is performed by the submit agent).
  - If the agent finds the submit agent (waiting in a goal area), move to place the attachment(s) as described by the task plan to form the final pattern.
  - If the agent is the submit agent, move towards a goal area.
  - If not the submit agent and believe that submit agent is in a goal area, move towards the position of the submit agent.
  - If a goal area is known, move towards it (to see if we can find the submit agent there).
  - Move into the most promising direction based on the exploration heuristics.
- If the agent is not selected to hand in any task (not part of the current task plan)
  - If a block or dispenser is in vision:
    * Rotate such that a free attachment spot is facing the direction of the block/dispenser. If rotation is blocked, move.
    * If it is a block, attach it to the agent.
    * If it is a dispenser, request a block.
    * If not next to the block, move towards it.
  - Move into the most promising direction based on the safe exploration heuristics.
- Perform *skip* action.

Your agents only got local perceptions of the whole scenario. Did your agents try to build a global view of the scenario for a specific purpose? If so, describe it briefly. No global view is attempted beyond the position of other agents in the team.

How do your agents decide which tasks to complete? Based on the currently collected blocks.

Do your agents form ad-hoc teams to complete a task? Yes, see above.

Which aspect(s) of the scenario did you find particularly challenging? The random map change events and deciding which blocks to clear (ultimately, we avoided trying to clear blocked paths).

If another developer needs to integrate your techniques into their code (i.e., same programming language tools), how easy is it to make that integration work? That entirely depends on the programming language. Prolog is deeply integrated into much of the code.

A.5   And the moral of it is ...

What did you learn from participating in the contest? We learned about using GOAL and general training in solving complex problems with no obvious solution.

What are the strong and weak points of your team? Our agents are rather flexible and rarely idle. Weak points are that we are possibly too greedy collecting blocks which makes it harder to navigate the map as the simulation progresses.

Where did you benefit from your chosen programming language, methodology, tools, and algorithms? GOAL helps our agents become flexible. We are forced to think in moment-to-moment reasoning and not just plans.

Which problems did you encounter because of your chosen technologies? The freedom can make it harder to keep things simple as the complexity grows. Furthermore, GOAL had some integration issues with the provided EIS interface. We have to attempt changes to the source code to run.

Did you encounter new problems during the contest? We were unaware of the feature that allows for multiple simulations without restarting. Furthermore, we had not tested GOAL with very fast simulations (the fact that we did not sent idle actions in our testing created an artificial slowdown).

Did playing against other agent teams bring about new insights on your own agents? We learned that with another team playing the map became even harder to navigate based on our approach. However, we probably also won some matches by creating the same problem for the opponent.

What would you improve (wrt. your agents) if you wanted to participate in the same contest a week from now (or next year)? Less rigid task submission plans and a less greedy approach to mindlessly collecting all blocks possible.

Which aspect of your team cost you the most time? Navigating the map and trying to make the agents find each other for submission.

What can be improved regarding the contest/scenario for next year? Set up test matches early using the contest setup to discover technical difficulties.

Why did your team perform as it did? Why did the other teams perform better/worse than you did? We did not use roles for agents to help with different tasks. We saw other teams using interesting strategies to solve the tasks. Ultimately, we also had some false assumptions about the scenario which created artificial problems that could have been avoided. In the end, some parts of the design should be completely redone.

References

1. Hindriks, K.V., de Boer, F.S., van der Hoek, W., Meyer, J.-J.C.: Agent programming with declarative goals. In: Castelfranchi, C., Lespérance, Y. (eds.) ATAL 2000. LNCS (LNAI), vol. 1986, pp. 228–243. Springer, Heidelberg (2001). https://doi.org/10.1007/3-540-44631-1_16
2. Hindriks, K.V.: Programming rational agents in GOAL. In: El Fallah Seghrouchni, A., Dix, J., Dastani, M., Bordini, R.H. (eds.) Multi-Agent Programming, pp. 119–157. Springer, Boston (2009). https://doi.org/10.1007/978-0-387-89299-3_4
3. Hindriks, K.V., Dix, J.: GOAL: a multi-agent programming language applied to an exploration game. In: Shehory, O., Sturm, A. (eds.) Agent-Oriented Software Engineering, pp. 235–258. Springer, Heidelberg (2014). https://doi.org/10.1007/978-3-642-54432-3_12
4. Boss, N.S., Jensen, A.S., Villadsen, J.: Building multi-agent systems using Jason. Ann. Math. Artif. Intell. **59**, 373–388 (2010)
5. Vester, S., Boss, N.S., Jensen, A.S., Villadsen, J.: Improving multi-agent systems using Jason. Ann. Math. Artif. Intell. **61**, 297–307 (2011)
6. Ettienne, M.B., Vester, S., Villadsen, J.: Implementing a multi-agent system in python with an auction-based agreement approach. In: Dennis, L., Boissier, O., Bordini, R.H. (eds.) ProMAS 2011. LNCS (LNAI), vol. 7217, pp. 185–196. Springer, Heidelberg (2012). https://doi.org/10.1007/978-3-642-31915-0_11
7. Villadsen, J., Jensen, A.S., Ettienne, M.B., Vester, S., Andersen, K.B., Frøsig, A.: Reimplementing a multi-agent system in Python. In: Dastani, M., Hübner, J.F., Logan, B. (eds.) ProMAS 2012. LNCS (LNAI), vol. 7837, pp. 205–216. Springer, Heidelberg (2013). https://doi.org/10.1007/978-3-642-38700-5_13
8. Villadsen, J., et al.: Engineering a multi-agent system in GOAL. In: Cossentino, M., El Fallah Seghrouchni, A., Winikoff, M. (eds.) EMAS 2013. LNCS (LNAI), vol. 8245, pp. 329–338. Springer, Heidelberg (2013). https://doi.org/10.1007/978-3-642-45343-4_18
9. Villadsen, J., From, A.H., Jacobi, S., Larsen, N.N.: Multi-agent programming contest 2016 - the Python-DTU team. Int. J. Agent-Orient. Softw. Eng. **6**(1), 86–100 (2018)
10. Villadsen, J., Fleckenstein, O., Hatteland, H., Larsen, J.B.: Engineering a multi-agent system in Jason and CArtAgO. Ann. Mathe. Artif. Intell. **84**, 57–74 (2018)

The Requirement Gatherers' Approach to the 2019 Multi-Agent Programming Contest Scenario

Michael Vezina$^{(\boxtimes)}$ and Babak Esfandiari$^{(\boxtimes)}$

Carleton University, Ottawa, ON, Canada
michaeljvezina@cmail.carleton.ca, babak@sce.carleton.ca

Abstract. The 2019 Multi-Agent Programming Contest (MAPC) scenario poses many challenges for agents participating in the contest. We discuss The Requirement Gatherers' (TRG) approach to handling the various challenges we faced—including how we designed our system, how we went about debugging our agents, and the strategy we employed to each of our agents. We conclude the paper with remarks about the performance of our agents, and what we should have done differently.

1 Introduction

Each year, the Multi-Agent Programming Contest (MAPC)[1] releases a scenario that discusses the specifics of the contest. The scenario goes into depth about the simulation environment, the perceptions and actions available to each agent, and the requirements that the agents must satisfy in order to perform well in the contest.

We introduce the paper with a brief description of the 2019 MAPC scenario. We then go on to discuss the specifics of the The Requirement Gatherers' (TRG) team, starting with the design challenges and motivations that drove the main system design decisions. The design decisions that were made are then discussed in detail, including the purpose of each of the individual system components, the interactions between them, and the purpose they serve in the system. The various setbacks encountered with debugging our multi-agent system are discussed, along with the various approaches used. We introduce a visualization tool that helped significantly with debugging our agents when used in tandem with the standard agent debugging tools.

The team strategy section will look at the main behaviour and strategy of the various agent roles, and what part each of them play in the overall simulation. We then conclude the paper with some remarks about TRG's performance in the competition, using the gathered agent metrics to help speculate why the team performed the way that it did.

---

[1] https://multiagentcontest.org/.

© Springer Nature Switzerland AG 2020
T. Ahlbrecht et al. (Eds.): MAPC 2019, LNAI 12381, pp. 106–150, 2020.
https://doi.org/10.1007/978-3-030-59299-8_5

1.1   The 2019 Scenario: Agents Assemble

The MAPC scenario varies from year to year, this year (2019) the scenario is named "Agents Assemble". Two teams are placed on a map represented by a rectangular grid and are required to complete tasks by their respective deadlines to compete for the most points. Each agent is provided with a list of tasks to be completed, and can collaborate with their team to determine which task to complete and how a given task can be completed.

The scenario places a lot of limitations on the agents, including a (severely) limited perception range, lack of agent identification perceptions, events that destroy and regenerate areas of the map, among other additional limitations. We will discuss all of the limitations and challenges faced, and our solutions to them, in detail throughout this paper.

2   System Design: Challenges and Motivations

Jason[2] [1] is an AgentSpeak(L) [2] interpreter built on Java that was made specifically for the development of multi-agent systems. Jason provides various agent-oriented features on top of its ability to interpret AgentSpeak code. Jason does all of the heavy-lifting with regards to how the agents reason, while also allowing the agent developer to customize any aspect of the architecture. On top of this, Jason also provides the ability to specify an agent environment, customize various selection functions, and allows for the calling and exchanging of information to (and from) Java code through the usage of internal action functions.

The general system design approach for this team is to use AgentSpeak code for the implementation of agent behaviour and strategy, using Jason to provide its powerful interpreting, reasoning, and customization abilities. The AgentSpeak code will utilize Jason's internal actions to defer to Java code when it is necessary or more convenient to do so. This section first introduces Jason's internal actions and how we plan on using them in our system. Following that, we discuss some of the design concerns that were encountered during the process of agent development.

2.1   Jason Internal Actions and Their Usage

We make extensive use of Jason's internal actions in our system due to the required interaction of components that exist both within the AgentSpeak and Java realms of our codebase. To ensure the reader understands the context behind how and why internal actions are used in our system, we will provide a brief description of internal actions and how they can be defined and used by the agents.

---

[2] http://jason.sourceforge.net/.

An internal action is a Java class that implements Jason's InternalAction interface (or extends the DefaultInternalAction class). By implementing this interface, our internal action class is recognized by Jason and can be called by the agent from within AgentSpeak. Internal actions act as a bridge between Java and AgentSpeak code, and can be utilized to invoke functionality and transfer data from AgentSpeak to Java (or vice-versa). To demonstrate why this may be useful (or even required in some cases), consider the following example. In our system, we rely on a Java A* implementation to generate a path for the agent so that it may navigate to its destination. We need to invoke the path generation functionality from AgentSpeak but our A* path-finding algorithm can only be accessed through its respective Java object. In order to achieve this, we must bridge this gap by invoking this functionality through the usage of internal actions.

Internal actions are invoked in AgentSpeak by specifying the Java package and class name of the internal action class. Given our path-finding example above, let's assume that we have a Java class named "internal.find_path" (shown in Listing 1.1) that invokes the A* path-finding algorithm. AgentSpeak code that executes this internal action is shown in Listing 1.2. In the listing, we can also see that the internal action arguments are Jason literals that can be used for both input and output. The first term is the agent's desired destination and the second term is unified by the internal action function to provide a path to the agent. In AgentSpeak, after the internal action is executed, the "Path" term is unified with a path to the specified destination.

Throughout our system (and this paper), we utilize internal actions to allow our agents to communicate with, and take advantage of, Java components and functionalities from within AgentSpeak.

Listing 1.1. Shows an example implementation of an internal action that invokes a path-finding algorithm.

```
package internal;
public class find_path extends DefaultInternalAction {
    @Override
    public Object execute(TransitionSystem ts, Unifier un,
        Term[] args) throws Exception {
        // Get destination and find path
        Term destTerm = args[0];
        Term pathTerm = executeAStar(destTerm);
        // Unify obtained path with argument Path term.
        un.unifies(args[1], pathTerm);
        // Return true for success
        return true;
    }
}
```

Listing 1.2. An example of using an internal action in AgentSpeak to find a path to location (0, 1) using A*

```
+!getPath
   :  // Call internal action that unifies Path with the path
      internal.find_path(dest(0, 1), Path)
   <- // Follow the given path
      !followPath(Path).
```

2.2 A High-Level Overview of Our Approach

We will briefly describe the approach that our team took to break down the different challenges faced throughout the course of the competition. Figure 1 shows a high-level diagram detailing the main system components and how the behaviour of our agent interacts with these components. The usage of these high-level components by the agent with respect to its specific goals and plans will be discussed in detail in the team strategy section.

Our team of agents utilizes a coordinate and navigation system with a data structure—known as the map model—that stores the map knowledge of each agent as they perceive the map. These components are the main building blocks that allow the agents to navigate and reason about their map knowledge. The agents also utilize the coordinate system as a basis for unique agent identification. As each agent moves around the map and perceives other team agents, they will attempt to determine the identity of one another. Identification allows the identified agents to collaborate and share information with each other. The updating of the map model, and the agent identification process, occurs asynchronously from any other tasks being carried out by the agent.

In the team strategy section, we demonstrate how the agents can then use the high-level system design components to fulfill their immediate goals and ultimately complete tasks in the simulation. Agents who work on the tasks are called *builders*. The builders are assigned tasks in sub-teams. One builder in the sub-team is assigned the status of the *master builder*, and acts as a centralized point to coordinate, connect, and submit the requirements. The other builders (the *slave builders*) are responsible for obtaining their respective blocks from dispensers, and then delivering and connecting their block to the master builder. Once all task requirements have been connected, the master builder can submit the task on a goal space.

Although the navigation, coordinate, map model, and identification components do not constitute the complete system, we demonstrate the purpose of these main components and how the agents interact with them in Fig. 1. This is a high-level diagram showing the main questions that each component can answer.

Some of the design challenges that we faced stemmed from certain limitations in Jason and multi-agent system development in general; these are discussed in

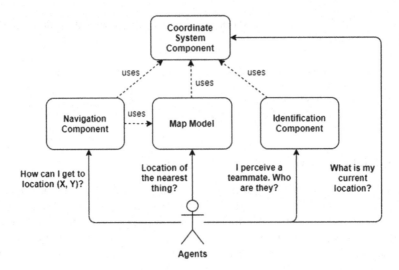

Fig. 1. A high-level diagram showing some of the main system components. The dependencies of each component are shown with dashed lines, and the questions that each agent may ask the component are in bold. The agents actor is meant to demonstrate how the behaviour of the agent (implemented in AgentSpeak) interacts with these main components to form the basis of its strategy.

the general software engineering design concerns. The other concerns we faced were due to intentional limitations put in place by the MAPC scenario; these will be discussed separately from the general software engineering design concerns. Each section will discuss its relevant design concerns and motivations, and will provide a list of design requirements in order to address the concern at hand.

2.3   General Software Engineering Concerns

The general software engineering concerns include some of the limitations that were encountered with agent development; these concerns and motivations are independent of the contest scenario limitations. These requirements were created to motivate the proper design of our system, and are driven by factors such as requiring agent-specific information (such as agent perceptions) both within the AgentSpeak code (for the strategy implementation) and within the Java code (for Java-based components such as the A* navigation component).

Throughout the following subsections we discuss how these requirements are relevant, and how they help us develop agents that are modular and performant. The requirements extracted from the concerns discussed in the subsection are as follows:

1. Requiring access to readily-available agent state information from outside the agent code
2. Ensuring a proper separation of concerns between the agent code and any operations delegated to outside of the agent code

3. Ensuring proper synchronization between the agent reasoning cycle and the simulation cycles

Agent State Information Access. Components such as the map model and navigation system constantly need access to agent-specific state information, specifically the agent's map perceptions, outside of the AgentSpeak code. These components are accessed by the agents through internal actions. One method of providing agent-specific state information to the components is to retrieve the necessary information from the provided agent's transition system. The transition system is part of Jason's architecture and provides access to various agent information, including the current state of its perceptions and beliefs.

Unfortunately, the transition system does not provide a hassle-free way to quickly access state information. More often than not, iteration and type-casting are required before you are able to make any use of the information provided by the transition system. This is demonstrated in Listing 1.3, where we show how the transition system can be used to obtain and process information about all block perceptions.

The additional overhead associated with using the transition system is necessary in order to perform any processing on the current agent state perceptions. Every time an internal action is called, the code shown in Listing 1.3 is executed. Internal actions can be invoked many times during the deliberation stage; requiring iteration and type-casting every time they get called. This can have a significant impact on agent performance, reliability, and modifiability.

For reference, the components that we introduce in this paper result in the code shown in Listing 1.4. These listings demonstrate how the usage of agent containers and percept objects (both of which will be discussed in detail in future sections) can significantly reduce the performance impact on an agent when compared to the traditional approach of using the transition system and belief base. This is achieved by reducing the amount of querying, iterating, and parsing necessary to obtain this same information from the belief base. Additionally, since the agent container and percept objects contain relevant methods that provide access to the data and logic pertaining to the relevant percept, this significantly improves the readability and maintainability of the internal action code.

Our system looks to avoid the various performance-related issues that come with obtaining data directly from the transition system and belief base. To achieve this, we would like to introduce the following design requirements that aim to address these concerns:

1. A container for the current state of each agent that exposes an interface allowing for the querying of agent state information. The amount of type-casting required in order to process the information provided by this container should be minimized.
2. This container should process any new perceptions only once per simulation step.

3. A way to access the above-specified containers. This should be accessible by both the internal action classes and the environment class.
4. In order to further improve agent performance, the parsing and processing of percepts done by the container should be done on its own thread to minimize the impact on the agent threads.

Listing 1.3. Accessing agent state information from the transition system within an internal action. Most of this is boilerplate code.

```
Literal desiredPercept = ASSyntax.parseLiteral("thing(X, Y,
    block, Details)");

// Use pattern matching to find the desired perception
ts.getAg().getBB().getCandidateBeliefs(desiredPercept, un)
    per -> {
        // Return if not a percept (no percept source)
        if(!perLiteral.hasSource(
            ASSyntax.createAtom("percept")))
            return;

        // Only way to retrieve percept info.
        // Smelly: type-casting and term indices.
        NumberTerm xTerm = (NumberTerm) per.getTerm(0);
        NumberTerm yTerm = (NumberTerm) per.getTerm(1);
        Term typeTerm = per.getTerm(2);
        Term detailsTerm = per.getTerm(3);
        try {
            // Resolve and cast the coordinates
            int x = (int) xTerm.solve();
            int y = (int) yTerm.solve();

            // Obtain block details
            String thingType = typeTerm.toString();
            String details = detailsTerm.toString();

            // Process the percept information
            processBlock(x, y, details);
        } catch (NoValueException noValEx)
        { ... } // NumberTerm.solve() failed
    });
```

Listing 1.4. This shows how the agents can access state information from an Agent-Container object within an internal action. The AgentContainer provides direct and instant access to the perceptions without having to query, iterate, and parse unrelated perceptions in the belief base.

```
// Get name of agent that is calling the internal action
String agentName = ts.getAgArch().getAgName();

// Get SPW instance
SynchronizedPerceptWatcher watcher =
    SynchronizedPerceptWatcher.getInstance();

// Obtain the relevant container object from the SPW instance
AgentContainer container =
    watcher.getAgentContainer(agentName);

// Iterate all things currently perceived by the agent
// Provides instant access to perceived things
for(Thing thing : container.getPercepts().getThingList())
{
    // Only process block type (sub-class of Thing)
    if(thing instanceof Block)
        // Process the block (no parsing necessary)
        processBlock(thing.getX(), thing.getY(),
            thing.getDetails());
}
```

Separation of Concerns. The ability to call custom internal action functions within the AgentSpeak code in Jason allows the agents to utilize Java to implement some unit of functionality for the agent. The internal actions have access to all agent information, allowing the internal actions to make any necessary calculations or decisions based on the current agent state. However, it can be easy to rely on the internal actions to implement agent behaviour or logic that should typically be done through AgentSpeak. In this case, you may be losing out on the following potential benefits of Jason.

Jason provides various mechanisms for agents in a dynamic environment. The ability to specify contingency plans in Jason allow the agents to manage, or even rectify, failures or unexpected states caused by any agent, or the environment. As part of each reasoning cycle, Jason will ensure that the agent is performing its most desirable intentions—taking the current agent beliefs and environment perceptions into account. This means that the agents may drop its current intentions at any point in time, in order to pursue a goal or desire of higher importance. On top of this, Jason is inherently event-based, which allows the agent to manage events and perceptions as they are received from the environment.

The moment that strategy is implemented using internal actions rather than being expressed through Jason plans, the agents lose out on Jason's innate ability to re-evaluate the agent's goals and handle other current events occurring within the dynamic environment. Internal actions are treated as atomic operations with respect to the reasoning cycle. They have their place, which is to process information and provide a result, provide the agent with information not available through percepts (for example, using the map model to obtain data from outside the agent's perception range), or to provide a way of interfacing with higher-level components (such as utilizing the navigation system's path-finding algorithm).

By maintaining a proper separation of concerns, we can ensure that the reasoning mechanisms provided by Jason are being used to their full potential, while also making appropriate use of internal actions when necessary. Our agents attempt to use their immediate perceptions as much as possible, only deferring to internal actions when it is more appropriate or convenient.

This can be seen in the case of agent navigation. Agents will use the navigation system to find something on the map. However, since the map model used by the navigation system may be out of date, the path returned by the navigation system may not be accurate. The agent still utilizes the path, but uses its immediate perceptions to confirm whether or not the returned path is blocked. During navigation, if the immediate perceptions contradict or block the path returned by the navigation system, the agent will request a new path.

Reasoning Cycle. For the competition, it was desirable for the agents to perceive, think, and act asynchronously from the server. This means that an agent is allowed to perceive and deliberate multiple times per simulation step, until it decides on an action to perform. Once an action is performed and sent to the server, the agent waits until the beginning of the next simulation step before continuing onto its next reasoning cycle. Having the agents perceive and deliberate asynchronously from the simulation allows the agents to process multiple aspects of their current environment. Additionally, since the reasoning cycle of the agent typically executes much faster than one simulation step, the agents should never fall behind on the perceptions they are reasoning about. This prevents the agents from reasoning about stale information.

In contrast, if the reasoning cycle was synchronized with the simulation step (i.e. one agent reasoning cycle per simulation step) this would introduce contention between the various events that need to be processed by the agent; only one event can be processed per reasoning cycle and simulation step. This means that the agent must choose between handling incoming messages from other agents, handling belief base events (such as the addition and removal of beliefs), and executing its current intentions. All of these events must be processed within the span of a simulation cycle, therefore driving the requirement for having the agents reason asynchronously from the simulation. For example, let's say that an agent is executing a plan that navigates the agent to a specific destination. If the agent receives a message from another agent while executing this plan, the agent will have to choose between executing the navigation plan and processing the received message event. Both of these events require one reasoning cycle to process, and so processing one of these events essentially causes the agent to neglect processing the other event. This means that the agent may not be able to process all necessary information pertaining to the current simulation step, and therefore may not be able to decide on the best action (or in some cases, any action) to execute in the simulation.

2.4   MAPC Scenario-Specific Design Concerns

This section discusses some of the design concerns introduced by the 2019 "Agents Assemble" scenario. These concerns stem from the limited perception range and map information provided to agents, randomized map destruction and regeneration (clear events), not being able to uniquely identify teammates through perceptions, and not being able to rely on the provided perceptions to determine the current agent's attachments.

Each of the following sections will discuss the challenges imposed by the scenario, and the design requirements that need to be met in order to bridge some of the gaps and provide a system that allows agents to reason and act as reliably as possible in their environment.

Navigation Challenges. The simulation provides the agents with no information about their current location, no information about the map boundaries, and, on top of this, the simulation also restricts the perception range of the agent's map surroundings. The limited perceptions that are given to the agent are provided relative to the agent's location.

This makes navigation not only difficult, but also unreliable, due to each agent having a restricted view of the map and the fact that the map is extremely dynamic in nature. The agents use a path-finding algorithm in order to provide best-effort navigation. The agents must have some contingencies in place, just in case the dynamic environment causes the path-finding algorithm to provide a non-navigable path. Figure 2 shows the limited perception range of each agent, limited to within the blue bounding box.

In order for the agents to navigate as reliably as possible, we develop a best-effort navigation system that uses the A* path-finding algorithm. In order to utilize A* and optimize the path provided by the algorithm, the following requirements must be met:

1. A* operates on the agent's current map knowledge. We must maximize the agent's amount of up-to-date map knowledge to provide the best possible navigation path.
2. A* requires the map to be represented as a graph, with nodes and edges representing the possible paths the agent can take. This means that map knowledge must be processed and provided as a graph, and that the interaction between an agent and the map elements must be properly modelled through the edges between navigable nodes.
3. Map knowledge is constantly updated, and so adding new map knowledge to the graph should be as quick as possible. The graph should be initialized at the beginning of the simulation, and updated every new simulation step.

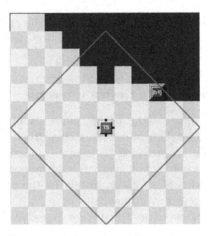

Fig. 2. The limited perception range of each agent. The agent only receives perceptions from within the blue bounding box. This image was captured from the simulation monitor. (Color figure online)

4. Since the path-finding algorithm will have to rely on outdated information outside of the agent's perception range, agents must be able to handle cases where the path given by the path-finding algorithm is blocked or inaccurate. The agent must be able to detect when the provided path is no longer valid and must be able to handle this.

Coordination Challenges. Agent coordination, which includes information sharing and task collaboration, is also made complicated by the simulation. On top of not being able to access any form of absolute positioning, agent teammates are also not uniquely identified by perceptions. To demonstrate, if the teammates agent T1 and agent T2 are within each other's range of perception, neither agent will receive any information regarding the identity of the other agent, except for the fact that they are teammates. This means that agent T1 does not know if the agent it is perceiving is agent T2, or if it is a different teammate (maybe it is agent T3). This becomes an issue specifically when agents are required to collaborate on tasks in the simulation.

In order to connect blocks together to satisfy task requirements, agents must use the *connect* action. The connect action allows two agents to connect two blocks together. When using the connect action, each agent must specify the name of the other agent it wishes to connect blocks with. Due to this, the agents must uniquely identify each other in order to perform any level of collaboration.

Although not a necessity, it would be in our best interest if agents could utilize identification to enable information sharing. Sharing information between agents would ensure that agents could collaborate more consistently and effectively, and would also require less time exploring the map since they could combine their map knowledge. In order to communicate knowledge between two agents, they must be able to uniquely identify each other while also providing a basis for communicating relative information (specifically, the map knowledge for each agent). In order to achieve agent coordination, the following requirements must be met:

1. There must be a mechanism to uniquely identify teammate agents
2. There must be a way to share information (including location information) between agents without the need for absolute coordinates from the simulation

Attachment Monitoring. The attachment perceptions provided by the simulation are generic and unreliable for identifying which agent the thing (such as a block or another agent) is attached to. For the sake of simplicity, the agents will only care about attached blocks (and will not pay any attention to any agents attached to each other).

The attached percept only provides information about the relative X and Y coordinate of the attached block and will not identify the agent that is attached to the block—even if the block is attached to the current agent. This means that agents must put further measures in place in order to keep track of the blocks they have attached to themselves.

The agents must be able to reliably keep track of their current attachments, as it allows them to determine whether or not they have the required blocks to complete tasks. Through attachment monitoring, the agents can detect if they lose an attachment and handle this scenario as appropriately and quickly as possible. Attachment monitoring also helps to accurately determine the movement and rotation directions that are blocked by attached blocks. This is used in navigation to determine which movement and rotation directions are unblocked. This ultimately helps reduce the amount of steps an agent may waste trying to move or rotate in a direction that is blocked by an attachment.

Requirement Planning. The requirements for each task in the simulation must be connected in a sequential order, otherwise it becomes impossible for agents to connect some of the requirements. The simulation does not provide the task requirements in any specific order, so we require an algorithm that plans out the task requirements, allowing the agents to connect the blocks in the required order.

Figure 3 shows an L-shaped task. In the case of the figure, the requirement planning algorithm would have to return the sequence as follows: requirement b1 at $(0, 1)$, requirement b0 at $(0, 2)$, and then requirement b0 at $(1, 2)$. Looking at this figure, it is easy to see that it would be impossible to connect the b0 block at $(1, 2)$ before the b0 block at $(0, 2)$.

As we discuss the overall system design and how it supports our team strategy in the upcoming section, we utilize these design concerns and motivations, and the introduced design requirements, to justify the main system design decisions that were made.

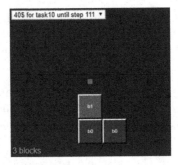

Fig. 3. An example of a task generated by the simulation. The red square represents the location of the agent, with respect to the attachments. This image was collected from the simulation monitor. (Color figure online)

3   System Design

The design of the system aims to address both the software engineering and MAPC scenario-specific design concerns mentioned in the previous section. We will introduce the various components of the system, how they interact with each other, and how they solve the various design concerns. The team strategy and agent behaviour implemented in AgentSpeak will be discussed in the team strategy section. This section mainly discusses the high-level system components that provide a basis for the agent behaviour to build off of. The components discussed in this section are built in Java, and are accessed by the agents through the usage of internal actions.

3.1   General System Design

This section discusses the main components and their interactions of the system. These components interact with one another in order to address the general software engineering concerns as a whole. The components in this section are the synchronized percept watcher, the agent containers, and the parsed percept objects. Figure 4 shows the general structure of each of these components, and Fig. 5 shows the interaction between these system components. These system components process and parse the raw percepts provided by the simulation into usable and readily-accessible information through the usage of various objects. As a whole, these components work together to make information access straightforward, while also doing it in a way that minimizes the performance impact on the agent threads.

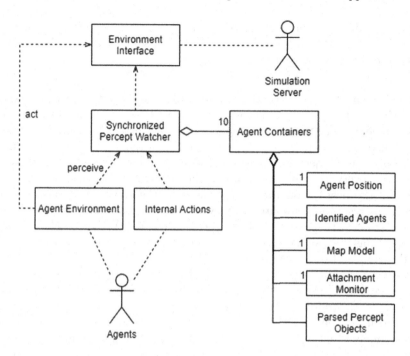

Fig. 4. The structure of each of the high-level components and how the agent interacts with them. The strategy of the agents, which is discussed in detail in the team strategy section, is represented by the agents actor.

Synchronized Percept Watcher (SPW). The synchronized percept watcher (SPW) is one component responsible for addressing some of the design concerns stated in the previous section. The SPW is a layer implemented in Java and sits between the competition-provided environment interface (EI) object (which communicates with the server directly), and the agent threads. It runs on its own thread, and polls the EI object for new agent percepts. Upon receiving new percepts, the SPW will parse and process them into containers for each agent, appropriately named *agent containers*.

The SPW was designed to be thread-safe; any attempts to access an agent container before new percepts have been completely processed will be blocked until the container is ready. In most cases, the SPW thread can parse and process the perceptions before the agent threads attempt to use the containers. The SPW parses and processes the new percepts only once per simulation step, caching the resulting agent containers. The agent threads can access and utilize these containers as much as they need, without requiring the containers to re-process the information provided by the server. The SPW provides global access to the agent containers through its singleton instance. This means that both the agent environment class and the agent internal action classes have access to the current agent state through the containers.

Agent Containers. The agent containers were developed to provide a single object that contains all information about an agent. Each agent container contains the agent name, the current step percepts, the current location of the agent, the complete map model object, the collection of currently identified teammates, and various other objects. The agent containers are created and updated by the SPW. Upon every new set of perceptions, the SPW will call each agent container, passing in the new set of raw perceptions from the server. The container will parse the percepts and update all relevant information about the agent (such as the current virtual location of the agent on the map). Each agent container also maintains the raw perceptions received by the server so that they may be directly provided by the environment to the agent during its perceive cycle. The agent containers also provide access to higher-level information and processing on the percepts. This information and processing is only available to the agents through internal actions.

This can be seen with the map model contained within the agent container. The map model contains a representation of all perceived map information over the course of the simulation—this includes perceptions that are currently outside our vision range. The map model also allows us to perform complex operations on the data, such as path-finding and map synchronization with identified teammates. Any information stored in the agent container, such as the map model object, needs to be requested and transferred through internal actions.

Parsed Percept Objects. The agent container also contains a collection of various percept classes. For every percept an agent may receive, there is a corresponding Java object. Each raw percept received by the SPW is parsed into their relevant Java objects by the agent container. The percept classes were developed with the purpose of containing the parsed information from each percept, while also providing appropriately-named get methods to retrieve the information. For example, it is possible to obtain perceived terrain information through the agent container and the parsed percept objects without needing to find and parse the perception from a generic Literal object (as is required when accessing perception information through the transition system).

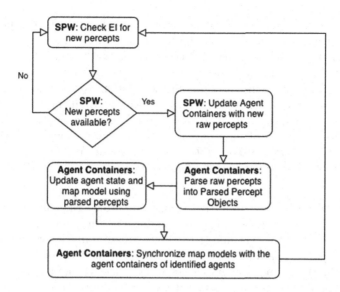

Fig. 5. A flowchart showing the general flow of information parsing and processing in the system, including how the agent containers are updated by the SPW.

Figure 5 shows how all of the system components interact with each other in order to update the agent state contained within the agent containers. The agent containers can be accessed from anywhere within the internal action or environment classes through the SPW singleton instance.

3.2 MAPC Scenario-Specific System Design

This section will discuss the design approach to dealing with all of the navigation requirements. This includes how the agents manage the limited perception range, incorporating a positioning system that can be used and understood by the agents, how map information is gathered and processed so that it may be usable by the navigation system, and how agents can use map information to intelligently explore the map and utilize the path-finding algorithm.

Virtual Absolute Positioning System. To help the agents make sense of their surroundings, we introduced a virtual positioning system. Each agent starts off with an initial position of $(0, 0)$, regardless of their actual location in the simulation. Successful move actions are used to update the agent's current location. This system provides an absolute location based off of the reference point of $(0, 0)$. Providing the agents with this positioning system allows them to keep track of map elements that are no longer part of their immediate perception range. The positioning system also helps form the basis of path-finding, since they can express destinations using virtual positions. Each location in the positioning system corresponds to one cell location on the simulation map.

The current virtual position of each agent is stored and updated by their respective agent containers. In order to provide the position information to the agents, the environment class will obtain the position from the container during the agent's perceive stage. Once obtained, the environment will provide the virtual position as a perception to the agent. The virtual position perception is one of the few pieces of information that is actually provided to the agent. This is because agents must be able to reason about their location, including determining whether or not path-finding is required.

The Map Model. Now that the agents can utilize the virtual positioning system in order to remember their surroundings as they navigate the map, we must create a structure that allows the agent to store and query the perceived map data. This map data must also be accessible in the form of a graph in order to be used by the A* algorithm. This is where the map model comes in. Each agent has their own map model, as it builds off of the virtual positioning system. The map model contains the graph object used for path-finding, and a list of current map perceptions.

After the agent containers parse the current perceptions, the container packages them up into corresponding *MapPercept* objects. Since it is possible to have multiple percepts corresponding to the same cell location on the map, the map model utilizes the MapPercept object to contain all percepts about a given cell. The map model creates one MapPercept object for each cell location in the perception range of the agent, and then places the perception information into the appropriate MapPercept object. Each MapPercept object contains the virtual position, the perceived terrain information, and a list of perceived things for its corresponding cell. The MapPercept object provides methods that determine how the current agent interacts with the terrain and things on that cell. These methods are utilized by the path-finding graph to model the possible agent movement with edges.

The map model contains all of the map data ever perceived by the agent. Since the positioning system is relative to each agent, it would not be possible for team agents to utilize the knowledge in each other's map model. This process of map model synchronization is possible once agents have uniquely identified each other, and can provide a way to translate knowledge between the two agent's coordinate systems.

Agent Identification. As a crucial component of team coordination, agents are required to identify one another. One of the many restrictions of the simulation is that agents can not perceive the specific identity of the agent. For example, assume we are agent T1 and we perceive two teammates: agent T2 and agent T3.

The perceptions provided to agent T1 specify the relative location and the team that agent T2 and T3 are on, but do not specify which perception corresponds to agent T2 and which corresponds to agent T3. This, in tandem with not knowing your absolute position in the simulation, makes it difficult for two agents to communicate directly and ultimately poses a major challenge for precise and reliable team coordination.

The process of agent identification starts off with each agent having no knowledge of other teammates. Upon perception of a team member, they will attempt to identify one another through a simple process that utilizes their relative coordinates. Upon perception of a teammate, both agents will broadcast the fact that they perceive a teammate to the *operator* agent. The operator is a Jason agent that centralizes team-wide tasks, such as task assignments and identification communications. The role of the operator agent will be discussed in more detail in the team strategy section, for now we simply recognize the operator as an agent that receives, processes, and sends out communications to and from each of the individual team agents.

It is now the job of the operator to determine whether or not the identity of a teammate perception is trivial. Agents perceive each other in pairs, if agent T1 perceives agent T2, then agent T2 will always perceive agent T1. The operator can use the perceived relative locations to deduce the identity of each agent in the pair, based off of the agents that broadcasted a message to the operator. If more than one pair of agents perceive each other at the same relative location, the operator is not able to deduce the identity of any of the agents in the pairs. If this is the case, the operator abandons the identification process, and the agents continue as if nothing happened. This process repeats every time agents perceive each other, so if identification fails, it is likely that the agents will eventually be able to identify one another in the near future. Once agents identify each other, they will be identified for the remainder of the simulation.

Upon successful identification between two agents, say agent T1 and agent T2, each agent calculates the *translation coordinates*. The translation coordinates correspond to the (X, Y) value that represent the difference between agent T1 and agent T2's virtual location of $(0, 0)$. The translation coordinates provide a way for identified agents to communicate virtual positions to one another, including meeting points (for task building and submission) and for sharing map information with each other, allowing them to synchronize their maps and contribute to a common map model.

3.3 Monitoring Agent Attachments

Since each agent must keep track of their own attachments, and are not able to rely on attach percepts, we must add a mechanism that keeps track of attached blocks in an intelligent way. This mechanism should update its model any time the agent attaches, detaches, or connects a block, which should be a simple task. However, it is also possible for blocks to be destroyed by clear events and task submissions.

To take care of this, we can create an internal model for each agent that contains a collection of all of the blocks attached to the agent. One thing to note, is that we make the assumption that we will never attach to another teammate. Although this is possible in the simulation, the agents proactively ensure that this never happens. Additionally, the agents ensure that they only attach and connect one block at a time. This makes the attachment model logic simple, yet accurate.

Any time the agent attaches, connects, or detaches a block, the agent updates the model through an internal action. To account for clear events, and task submissions, we allow the attachment model object to refresh itself at the start of every step. The model can utilize the absence of an attach percept to determine if we have lost an attachment. If the model thinks it has an attachment, but the simulation does not provide an attach percept, the model can safely remove the attachment. This handles the impact of an unexpected clear events and task submissions, and allows the model to maintain an accurate representation of what blocks are attached.

3.4   Task Requirement Planning

Each task is defined with the list of requirements necessary for successful task submission. Each requirement defines the block type and the required attached location of the block, relative to the submitting agent. In order to ensure that all requirements can be connected to the submitting agent, the requirements must be planned out.

Understanding Task and Requirement Generation. Each requirement is composed of an (X, Y) coordinate, and a block type. In order to ensure that agents can connect the generated task requirements, the simulation server generates the requirements in a specific sequence. We can utilize the same rules that the server uses to generate the requirements in order to plan out the proper sequence of requirement connections. The coordinate of the first requirement will always be $(0, 1)$, this is directly south of the attaching agent. Every requirement after that can only be south, east, or west of the previous requirement location. The simulation will never generate a requirement north of its predecessor.

We can exploit these rules in order to come up with the requirement sequence. We search through the list of unordered requirements looking for the requirement with a location of $(0, 1)$. Once found, we look for a requirement to either the east $(1, 1)$ or west $(-1, 1)$ side, and if one does not exist, we look south $(0, 2)$ for a requirement. We then repeat this for every requirement until we exhaust the list of requirements. The end result is an ordered list of requirements that the builder agents can use to build the tasks in the correct order. Figure 6 demonstrates this procedure through the usage of a flowchart.

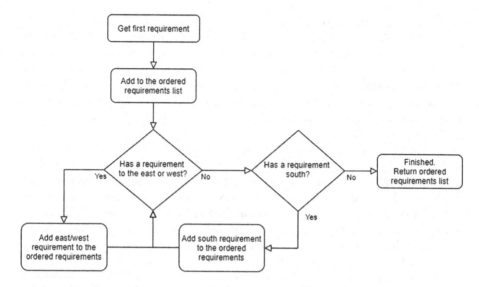

Fig. 6. A flowchart demonstrating how the ordered sequence of requirements is built from an unordered list.

4 Debugging

Most of the development time was spent on debugging unwanted agent behaviour. In some cases, the debugging tools that were used added more resistance to development and debugging efforts. One tool specifically—the agent mind inspector, which is a debugging tool provided by Jason—was very helpful during the initial stages of development, where there was only one agent in operation and the single agent had very simple behaviour. As soon as additional agents were introduced and the behaviour became more complex, debugging the agents using the mind inspector started to become a time-consuming and troublesome task. We needed to find a better solution to debugging the agents. This section will discuss the debugging techniques that were used during the course of agent development. This includes debugging efforts that involve the Jason mind inspector, the debugging support provided by the IntelliJ IDE[3], a custom-built agent state visualization tool, and some combination of all of the tools.

4.1 Jason's Mind Inspector

The Jason mind inspector provides the ability to debug and step through the behaviour of the agent. Unfortunately, debugging the behaviour of multiple agents using the mind inspector became a troublesome task as behaviour increased in complexity. When debugging using the Jason mind inspector, you

---

[3] https://www.jetbrains.com/idea/.

are able to pause and step through the execution of one or all of the agent reasoning cycles. Since the simulation executes separately from the agent threads, the simulation will continue its execution even though the agent threads are paused for debugging. This causes synchronization issues between the agents and the simulation, which in turn introduces other issues, making it difficult to trace down the root cause of the original bug. This is not an issue specific to Jason, or even multi-agent systems, but rather an inherent issue in debugging multi-threaded applications.

In an attempt to combat the synchronization issue, the mind inspector's "history" option was used. This option allows the inspector to keep a full history of all agent reasoning cycles. Using this option allows the developer to keep the agent threads running, while still providing a way for the developer to examine the recorded reasoning cycles and behaviour. Unfortunately, keeping a full history of every piece of information for each reasoning cycle quickly grew out-of-hand, causing the debugger to be sluggish and completely unusable. To make matters worse, the debugger would also slow down all of the agent threads, making the inspector's history option a dead-end. Breakpoints in Jason allow the debugger to run until a breakpoint (specified in the AgentSpeak code) is hit. Unless the "history" option is enabled, it is extremely difficult to determine the context of the current reasoning cycle, since you do not have a trace of how the agent got to the current state.

Since the debugging tools provided by Jason were designed for the specific purpose of debugging agent behaviour, they were limited to only being able to see the information available in the AgentSpeak code. If any bugs occurred with any of the Java components (such as the agent's container or the map model), the mind inspector would not be able to provide any insight. This is where IntelliJ's debugging support comes in.

4.2   IntelliJ IDEA IDE Debugging Support

IntelliJ, which is a Java IDE, provides some excellent tools and support for debugging Java applications. We can utilize the debugging tools provided by IntelliJ to help us debug our system. Debugging issues with any of the Java components was straight-forward, all that was required was setting a breakpoint and stepping-through the operation of the component. This method of debugging is still prone to the multi-threaded debugging issues, although this issue can be alleviated through the usage of conditional breakpoints. This allows us to debug the code when necessary (and only under certain conditions), and so getting out-of-sync with the simulation only occurs when the breakpoint gets triggered. At this point, if the agents get out-of-sync with the simulation, it typically doesn't matter since we have the relevant information required to examine the issue from the agent containers.

Although this method of debugging was less troublesome than the mind inspector, there was still a large amount of information that had to be processed in order to diagnose any issues. For example, there were initial issues with the virtual positioning system, but they did not express themselves until the agents had to perform path-finding on the map model. Because of all of the interactions between the components, this issue was very difficult to diagnose, even with IntelliJ's debugging support. On top of this, IntelliJ does not provide any support for debugging the agent's reasoning cycle.

4.3 Agent Visualization Tool

In order to help reduce the amount of effort that went into debugging, a custom visualization tool was created. This tool provides a visual representation of each agent's current state, providing full flexibility in the information that the tool can display. This tool provided a way to monitor the state of the agent. When any abnormalities were detected in either the behaviour of the agent or the information displayed by the tool, it was easy to pin-point the component that was causing the issue.

For example, the previously-mentioned issue relating to the virtual positioning system was quickly detected with the visualization tool. By having the visualizer show the agent's knowledge of the map as well as the current location of the agent, it was obvious that the virtual position was not updating in the correct circumstances—in this case, it was not updating correctly whenever the agent attempted to move into an obstacle. Without the visualization tool, a lot of breakpoints and stepping through execution would have been required to determine the root cause. The visualization tool shows everything about the agent: map information, the list of identified agents, the current navigation path of the agent, the current attached blocks, and more.

Figure 7 shows the information conveyed by the visualization tool. The figure shows the map knowledge as a collection of square cells. The different cell colours represent the various things or terrain. To name a few examples, the yellow cells are team agents, black cells are obstacles, pink cells are goal spaces, and the blue cells are block dispensers. The dark grey cells are the locations that the agent has not explored yet. The figure also shows the current simulation step information at the top left corner, along with a list of the team agents that have been identified by the current agent (and their current location on the map).

The visualization tool can be easily modified to add and remove basic information that is displayed on the window (such as a new type of map terrain). However, this tool is still an ad hoc solution that is specific to the TRG agents and the 2019 MAPC scenario. Future work could be done to generalize this tool for other agents and environments.

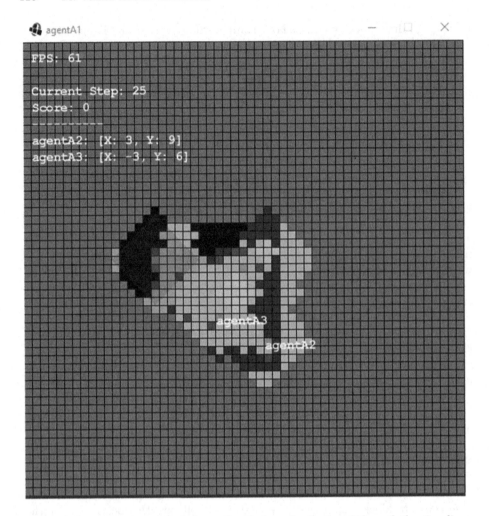

Fig. 7. A demonstration of the information that can be displayed through the visualization tool. One visualization tool window must be opened for each agent. This window shows the information contained by agent "agentA1". This agent window also happens to include information gathered by the agents "agentA2" and "agentA3", since both agents have been identified by agentA1. (Color figure online)

4.4   The Combined Approach

In the end, a combination of all three debugging approaches were used. The visualization tool was used to monitor both the Java and AgentSpeak components. Any time unwanted behaviour occurred, the visualization tool would provide enough information to create conditional breakpoints in IntelliJ, reducing the amount of guessing work and time required to pin-point the root of the bug. The visualizer was also used for debugging the behaviour implemented in AgentSpeak. Any time any strategic or behavioural issues were visually detected through the tool, we were able to invoke the Jason mind inspector at that moment in time in order to examine how the agent is reasoning. This tool ultimately reduced the amount of guess work involved in debugging the agents, and improved the debugging experience as a whole.

5 The Team Strategy

The team is composed of an operator and two main roles: the attackers, and the builders. The operator is a single agent that acts as a centralized point for assigning task requirements and processing agent identification notifications from other agents. The operator does not connect or perform in the simulation, but does communicate with the other agents. Out of the agents that do perform in the simulation, each agent is assigned either a role of attacker (also known as an offender), or builder. During the competition, agents T1 to T5 were builders, while agents T6 to T10 were assigned the attacker role. The attackers are agents that explore the map with the sole purpose of interfering with the other team. The builders are the agents who collaborate with one another in an attempt to build and submit tasks.

5.1 The Operator

The operator is an agent who does not participate in the simulation. Instead, the operator agent acts as a centralized point for processing team information, such as processing agent identification messages, monitoring currently assigned tasks, and assigning new tasks to *free agents*. The operator's role in agent identification has been previously discussed in the system design section, it simply just acts as a centralized point for organizing identification broadcasts into pairs based off of the relative location of perceptions. The operator then defers to an internal action to carry out further identification logic. This section focuses on the operator's role in selecting and assigning tasks to sub-teams of builder agents.

Listing 1.5 shows the AgentSpeak plan that the operator executes upon every new simulation step. This plan introduces the operator's desire to process the agent identification notifications (!processFriendlies), monitor the current task assignments (!updateTaskAssignments), and assign new tasks to free agents (!assignTasks).

Listing 1.5. The operator's plan for handling new simulation step events.

```
+step(CurStep)
    <- !processFriendlies(CurStep);
       !updateTaskAssignments;
       !assignTasks.
```

Task Assignment. The operator maintains a set of task assignment beliefs to keep track of each builder's current task assignment. Each belief takes on the form *taskAssignment(Agent, Task, Req)* where Agent is the builder agent name, Task is the assigned task name, and Req is a structure containing information about the assigned task requirement. On top of keeping track of the current task assignments, the operator also uses these beliefs to determine the free agents—the builder agents that are not in any current task assignment beliefs. As demonstrated by the structure of the belief, and as we will discuss, a builder will only be responsible for one requirement block for a given task.

The process of task assignment involves selecting a task and assigning it to a sub-team of free agents. The operator calls an internal action to help with the process of task selection and assignment. Since the internal action has access to the information in the agent containers, it can utilize the container information to determine the free agents that can communicate and collaborate on a task. The internal action iterates through the list of free agents provided by the operator, and checks if any of them have mutually identified one another. Sub-teams are then created based off of the mutually-identified agents, this guarantees that the agents are able to communicate and utilize the connect action with any other member of the sub-team. The internal action will attempt to maximize the number of agents in a sub-team, allowing it to take on larger tasks.

Once the sub-teams are determined, the internal action decides on a task assignment for the sub-team and assigns one requirement of that task to each sub-team member. Since each sub-team agent is responsible for only one requirement block, the sub-team can only be assigned a task that has a number of requirements less than or equal to the number of sub-team members. If a task is assigned to a sub-team, but has less requirements than the sub-team has members, any builders that are not assigned a requirement will remain free agents and will be removed from the sub-team.

If there are no free agents that have identified one another, no sub-teams or tasks will be assigned to the agents. It is also possible for multiple sub-teams to be formed, each will have their own mutually-identified members and unique task assignment. Once the internal action processes all of the free agents, it will return a list of all of the task and requirement assignments back to the operator. The operator will process each of the task and requirement assignments, and will add new task assignment beliefs to its belief base while also notifying any builders of their new task (and requirement) assignments.

Task Monitoring. Before performing the task assignment process, the operator will first update its list of current task assignments. The operator monitors each task assignment by iterating through each assignment belief and ensuring the assigned task is still valid. The task is considered valid if: 1. the task has not expired, and 2. the task has not yet been submitted by any team. If these conditions are not met, the operator will remove any task assignments associated with the invalid task and will notify any of the affected builders.

5.2   Shared Strategy Components

Despite the differences in strategy and behaviour, the attackers and builders share common elements and lower-level strategies in order to achieve their respective goals. Both roles, for example, will utilize some form of movement at some point in their lifetime, and it would be favourable to share some of the contingency plans associated with movement failure. It therefore makes sense to design and organize the AgentSpeak code in a way that maximizes the amount of code that can be utilized by both roles. Both roles share the same code base, the difference is that they have different goals that they aim to achieve.

Agent Identification. Both roles perform agent identification in order to share map knowledge, however, agent identification is crucial for builders as they require it to collaborate on tasks. The identification process is the same for all agents. Builders can identify and share information with the attackers, and vice-versa. Since we run the reasoning cycle asynchronously from the simulation cycle, this allows the agents to reason about multiple intentions, making it possible to handle and process multiple possible events such as agent identification and agent navigation, within one simulation step.

Navigation and Exploration. The navigation and exploration components provide the agent with plans for handling map navigation to a destination, searching for map things (dispensers, goal spaces, etc.), and intelligent map exploration. These components require access to the map model stored in the agent container object, therefore they all utilize internal actions to obtain their required information.

When searching for map things, the agent utilizes an internal action to query the map model for a specified thing. The internal action will return the virtual absolute location of the closest map cell that matches the request of the agent (for example, a dispenser), otherwise the internal action fails to unify if nothing in the map model matches the request. If nothing is found, the agent will explore the map until the internal action can resolve the request. If the map model can resolve the request and a virtual location is unified, the agent will utilize *destination navigation* to get to the unified destination.

The agents have the ability to explore the map in an intelligent way. Rather than aimlessly exploring in any given direction, the agents can utilize the map model to determine the closest missing chunk of the map. The closest missing map chunk is determined by finding locations that have not yet been perceived by the agent and obtaining the location with the smallest Euclidean distance from the agent's current location. The internal action for exploration unifies the best direction to explore in, in order to lead the agent to unexplored territory. This means that when an agent is exploring, they will almost always find new areas of the map with undiscovered things and terrain. Exploration is the default behaviour for all agents, they will explore the map until they have received enough information to achieve their respective goals. This means that a builder agent will explore the map until it identifies other builders, and perceives the relevant dispenser or block type in order to complete their assigned task. In the case of an attacker agent, they will continue exploring and navigating to different goal spaces until they find an enemy agent with an attached block located on a goal space.

Destination navigation utilizes path-finding on the map model to determine the shortest path from the agent's current location to a specified destination. The internal action will unify the path as a list of cardinal directions (N, S, E, W) that the agent must navigate in order to get to the destination. If the destination does not exist on the map model, or if there is no path to get to the destination, the destination navigation plan will fail. Jason will propagate this failure up the intention stack until a contingency is found to handle the failure. In cases where this happens, the agent typically will end up exploring until a path is available, but it is ultimately up to the implemented contingency plans to decide how to handle this failure.

If a path to the destination exists, the agent will follow the navigation path provided. If the next direction in the provided path is blocked (either by an obstacle or map things), or if the destination is not what the agent expected (the map got regenerated and caused the map model to be out-of-date), then the agent will call the path-finding internal action again. The internal action will determine the next best path to the destination, or will fail if none exists.

Action Plans and Contingency. Each scenario action (move, connect, attach, etc.) is managed by a plan in Jason. Each of these action plans have contingency plans in the case of any failures. They also provide some level of failure avoidance, implemented with respect to the action being performed.

To demonstrate this with the move action: if an agent were to attempt to move west, but one of its attachments is blocking movement, the move action plan will detect this and attempt to find a rotation where moving west is possible before it attempts the move action.

The move plan utilizes the canMove test goal shown in Listing 1.6 to rotate if our attachments are blocking movement. This test goal plan will rotate until the movement direction is no longer blocked. Once unblocked, the agent then performs the original move request.

Test goals are used in this way to bring the agent to a desirable and expected state in order to avoid failures. If a rotation can not be found and the movement can not be unblocked, the plan will fail and will propagate up to any parent intentions or contingency plans to handle.

Listing 1.6. Test goal to attempt to unblock the agent if the agent can not move

```
+?canMove(Dir)
  <- ?agentUnblocked(Dir); // Test if unblocked
     !resetExhaustedRotations; // Reset rotation attempts
     ?attachmentsUnblocked(Dir); // Unblocks attachments
     ?canMove(Dir). // Re-test current test goal
```

By avoiding and handling failures in this manner, we try to minimize the number of steps that the agents waste by sending actions that are guaranteed to fail or by being in a bad state. Jason's ability to manage failures through contingency plans definitely proved itself useful in this area, allowing us to capture and recover from various edge cases and bad states.

Getting Unstuck. While developing the agents, it was a common occurrence for the agents to be spawned in a location that was surrounded by obstacles. Without any mechanism for breaking out of this sort of situation, the agents essentially become useless for the rest of the simulation (unless they get lucky and an opposing agent or clear event clears up the obstacles for them). It is also possible for an agent to be blocked by things, such as another entity or a block. Both the attacker and builder agents utilize the same strategy in order to free themselves.

The agents will utilize an internal action in order to determine whether or not they are blocked in all directions (or "caged in"). The internal action will then determine the best obstacle to clear, which is determined as the obstacle with the highest number of surrounding free-spaces. By following this criterion, the agent can attempt to clear out a path that requires a minimal number of clear actions. Figure 8 demonstrates the strategy that the agents use to break out of their contained area.

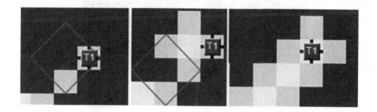

Fig. 8. The agent utilizes clear actions to break out of a contained space. The agent clears the obstacles that are most likely to open it up to free space.

5.3   Attacker Strategy

The attackers explore the map and utilize the clear action in order to interfere with the other team. When starting off, the attackers will explore the map until they discover any goal terrain. The attackers will then monitor the goal clusters by navigating to a known goal terrain location (including goal locations shared by the map knowledge of other agents). The attackers will look for opposing agents residing on a goal terrain that have at least one block attached to them, and will then use the clear action targeted at one of the attached blocks in an attempt to reject the opponent's potential task submission.

Listing 1.7 shows the clear action being executed by the attacker agent when an enemy is detected on a goal cell with an attached block. Figure 9 shows attacker agents T9 and T10 attacking opponent G3 in the first simulation against GOAL-DTU.

Listing 1.7. Search for perceived enemy and use clear action to attack the enemy.

```
+!searchForEnemy
   :  // Get perceived entity
      percept::thing(X, Y, entity, OtherTeam) &
      // Check that perceived entity is not our teammate
      not percept::team(OtherTeam) &
      // Check if we perceive a goal space:
      percept::goal(X, Y) &
      // And if the enemy entity has a block attached:
      hasBlockAttachedToEntity(X, Y)
   <- // Attack enemy at (X, Y):
      !clear(X, Y);
      // Search and attack again:
      !searchForEnemy.
```

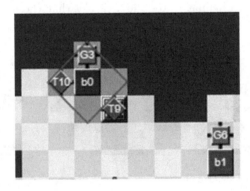

Fig. 9. Attacker agents T9 and T10 attacking opponent G3's block during simulation 1 of the match against GOAL-DTU.

5.4 Builder Strategy

The builders are responsible for performing the main scenario objective of requirement gathering, task building, and task submission. The builder agents separate this into multiple sub-goals. First, the builders explore the map while waiting for a task requirement assignment from the operator. After receiving an assignment, the builders will obtain their respective requirement blocks. Following this, the task's master builder determines a meeting point and communicates with each individual slave builder in order to sequentially deliver and connect each task requirement at the meeting point. Once all of the task requirements are connected, the master builder must submit the task.

Each of the sub-goals associated with fulfilling the task requirements have their own AgentSpeak plans. Each sub-goal plan must make sure that the builder successfully achieves the objective of the sub-goal. These plans also have their own respective contingency plans for managing and correcting any sub-goal-specific failures. If any of these sub-goal failures can not be managed or corrected by any of the contingency plans, the agent will detach any blocks and will re-attempt its current task requirement assignment from the start.

Free Agents: Waiting for a Task Assignment. When a builder is a free agent, it will wait for a task requirement from the operator. The builder has no other option but to explore the map in order to be somewhat productive, since it can't start working on a task yet. Exploring the map allows the builders to build on their current knowledge of the map while also identifying other agents on the team. As the number of mutually-identified free agents increases, the operator will be able to assign larger tasks to the sub-teams. By having a larger sub-team, the chances of being assigned a task will increase since you will be considered for a larger set of tasks.

Obtaining Block Requirements. When a new task assignment has been received, the builder will detach any existing attachments that are not relevant to the current requirement block type. When performing this, the builder will make sure it is outside of a goal cluster before detaching any blocks in order to prevent the detached block from cluttering up the goal space as a courtesy to both teams.

After detaching all irrelevant blocks, the builder will first check to see if it has the required block type already attached. If it does, the agent moves on to the next sub-goal (delivering the block). Otherwise, the agent must find a dispenser to obtain the block.

Listing 1.8 shows the obtainBlock plan for obtaining a given block type. Listing 1.9 shows the test goal plan that gets executed when the agent does not have the given block type attached to itself. This test goal is used by obtainBlock in order to ensure a block is attached before continuing.

Listing 1.8. Obtains a block of type Block. After successfully executing this plan, the agent is guaranteed to have a block attached to one of its sides.

```
+!obtainBlock(Block)
  <- // Tests if agent has block attached:
     ?hasBlockAttached(Block);
     // Unifies X, Y of attached block:
     ?hasBlockAttached(X, Y, Block);
     // Assert block location is a valid direction:
     ?xyToDirection(X, Y, Dir).
```

Listing 1.9. The test goal plan for when a block is not currently attached to the agent. The agent will search for the appropriate block dispenser, request a new block, and then attach it to itself.

```
+?hasBlockAttached(Block)
    <- // Find, dispense, and attach block from dispenser:
       !dispenseAndAttachBlock(Block);
       // Re-test goal:
       ?hasBlockAttached(Block).
```

When searching for the dispenser, the builder calls an internal action that provides the closest dispenser that dispenses the necessary block type (using A* to find the closest available dispenser). If the appropriate dispenser can not be found, the agent will explore until map knowledge of the required dispenser is introduced. When the appropriate dispenser is found, the agent will navigate to the dispenser, request the block from the dispenser, and attach the dispensed block to itself.

Delivering Blocks and Builder Coordination. Once the builders have the required block attached to themselves, they deliver the block to a common meeting point and connect their blocks to the other builders working on the same task. The sub-team responsible for each task will have one master builder, and multiple slave builders.

The master builder is the builder who was assigned the first ordered requirement—the requirement with a location of (0, 1). The rule responsible for determining this is provided in Listing 1.10.

Listing 1.10. The rule responsible for determining if the current agent's task assignment permits them to be the master builder.

```
isMasterReq(req(X, Y, _))
    :- X == 0 & Y == 1.
```

The master builder determines the meeting point for block delivery and connection for the sub-team, and also synchronizes the task requirement sequence with each slave builder. The slave builders—the builders responsible for all requirements that do not have a location of (0, 1)—will take turns delivering their attached blocks to the master builder. The master builder first navigates to the determined *meeting point*. The meeting point is where the slave agents will deliver and connect their block requirements with the master builder. The meeting point will always be on a goal terrain, and will be selected such that there is enough space below the master builder to connect the blocks from each slave.

Listing 1.11 demonstrates the plan that allows the master builder to coordinate with each slave. The master builder will coordinate the connection of the requirement blocks with the slaves. It utilizes the task requirement planning algorithm to determine the next slave that needs to deliver and connect their assigned requirement. The master builder will then notify the next slave builder that it must deliver and connect the requirement to the master, providing the slave with the destination location for the block. Slave builders that have attached their requirement block, but have not yet been notified by the master builder to deliver their requirement, will explore the map until they are notified.

Listing 1.11. The plan that allows the master builder coordinate with the slave builders.

```
+!informSlaves(Task)
   :  // Get the next task requirement:
      eis.internal.get_next_req(Task, PrevReq, Req) &
      // Unify the slave assigned to the requirement:
      taskAssignment(Slave, Task, Req)
   <- // Tell the slave that the meeting point has been set:
      .send(Slave, tell, meetingPointSet(Task));
      // Remove any previous attempts to connect for the task:
      .abolish(slaveConnect(Task, _)[source(_)]);
      // Prepare for connect syncing with slave
      !prepareForConnect(Slave);
      // Wait for a connect message from slave:
      !waitForConnect(Slave, Task, PrevReq, Req);
      // Repeat process for next requirement
      !informSlaves(Task).
```

Block Connection. As each slave gets notified to deliver their respective requirement block, they will navigate and rotate themselves in a way that ensures that the block is on the exact destination cell that the master builder requested. Once the block is on the specific destination, the slave builder will notify the master builder of the successful delivery. The master will then notify the slave that it is ready to connect, and both agents will attempt to connect their blocks. This behaviour is demonstrated by the AgentSpeak plan shown in Listing 1.12.

Listing 1.12. The plan that allows a slave builder to coordinate with the master builder.

```
+!deliverBlock(Task, Req)
   :  // Assert I am not a master
      not isMasterReq(Req) &
      // Check that the master has set my meeting point
      meetingPointSet(Task)[source(Master)] &
      // Get the meeting point for the slave
      eis.internal.get_slave_meeting_point(Master, Req,
   location(X,Y))
   <- // Bring block to meeting point
      !navigateBlock(Req, X, Y);
      // Connect the block with the master builder
      !slaveConnect(Master, Task, Req).
```

If the connect action fails unexpectedly, both agents will try the connection again on the next step. Upon successful block connection, the slave agent will detach itself from the connected block. The block delivery and connection process is then repeated with the slave builder responsible for the next requirement in the task. If all requirements have been connected, the master builder will proceed to task submission.

Task Submission. Since the master has already predetermined the meeting point of block delivery to be on a goal cell, the master can submit the task immediately after connecting all of the requirements with the slave builders. Once the master submits the task successfully, it will notify the operator. The operator will remove the relevant task and requirement assignment beliefs for the sub-team. Listing 1.13 shows the plan responsible for task submission.

Listing 1.13. When the master goes to inform the next slave, the context of this plan allows us to handle the case where we are done building the task. Since the meeting point for the builders requires that the master be on a goal space before building the requirements, we can attempt task submission since we will already be on a goal cell.

```
+!informSlaves(Task)
    :   // We have attached all blocks to the master agent
        eis.internal.get_next_req(Task, _, done)
    <- // Submit the task
       !performAction(submit(Task)).
```

In the next section, we discuss the performance of the TRG agents in the competition. We will use various metrics to help measure the effectiveness of each of the strategies discussed in this section, providing insight on what aspects of our team strategy went well and what could have been improved.

6   Agent Performance

The TRG team won 1 simulation, tied 2, and lost 6. In this section we analyze some of the match statistics, providing some speculation about the issues encountered by the agents during the competition and where things could have been improved. The data used for the metrics in this section were obtained from the competition match replays.

6.1   Match Performance Metrics

The performance of the team throughout the various matches can be examined through a total of 10 different metrics. Each of the metrics can be used to measure the performance of at least one aspect the agent strategy.

Metric 1: Attachment Utilization. The attachment utilization metric is used to show how many blocks were obtained, and how many of those obtained blocks were actually used in tasks. The only reason that the builders attach blocks is so that they can complete tasks. When this metric is low, this signifies that the builders are wasting time obtaining and attaching blocks. This metric is provided as the number of used attachments/the number of obtained attachments.

Metric 2: Number of Connections Made. The number of connections made is provided as a way to measure the number of successful block connections between builders. Successful connections demonstrate that the agents are able to collaborate correctly, this further measures the ability to perform block delivery and connection synchronization between the master and slave builders.

Metric 3: Submitted Tasks. This metric is the number of submitted tasks in the simulation. This measures the overall ability of the builders.

Metric 4: Failed Submissions. This is the number of failed submissions. A failed submission occurs when the agents gather and connect all of the block requirements, but fail to submit a task. This metric can signify issues with the builder task submission process, or an issue with the builder's ability to complete tasks before the deadline.

Metric 5: First Task Start Time. The first task start time is defined as the simulation step of the first block attachment used in the first task submission. This metric measures how quickly the agents can explore the map to identify one another, get assigned a task from the operator, and then attach the first task requirement block. This shows how long the agents take before getting starting on task building.

Metric 6: Average Task Requirement Size. This is the average number of requirements for all of the tasks submitted in a simulation. This measures the team's willingness and ability to complete larger tasks.

Metric 7: Average Task Completion Time (Per Requirement). The average task completion time measures the team's ability to complete tasks in a timely manner. This is calculated for each task by measuring the amount of time between the first block attachment, and the task submission time. This result is then divided by the number of task requirements so that the completion time is normalized to account for the task size.

Metric 8: Average Attach to Connect Time. After attaching a block to itself, the slave builders must then connect the block to the master builder. This metric, which measures the average time between block attachment and connection, shows how long the slave builders take to deliver and connect their blocks with the master builder. This metric is directly influenced by the distance between the location of the block dispenser—where the slave agent attaches the block requirement—and the meeting location set by the master agent— where blocks are delivered and connected. This metric is improved by choosing a meeting point close to the necessary block dispensers.

Metric 9: Average Last Connect to Submit Time. The average time between the last successful block connection and the task submission time is used to measure the amount of time the master builder spends getting to a goal space and submitting the task. As we will see in the match performance results, the master builders maintained a consistently low value for this metric. This is attributed to the meeting point selection algorithm, which always brings the master builder to a goal cell before the requirements are delivered and connected by the slave agents. Upon successfully building the task requirements, the master builder can immediately submit the task.

Metric 10: Opponent Rejected Submissions. This single metric is used to measure the performance of the attacker agents. This metric defines a "rejected submission" as a successful clear operation on an opposing agent who is located on a goal space with an attached block. The clear action will successfully disable the agent and will remove any of its attached blocks affected by the clear action.

For the clear action to be performed, it must be executed 3 steps in a row on the same space. Even if an opposing agent did not have the intention of task submission, we assume that since the agent was waiting with a block on a goal cell, it was somehow involved in the task submission process. By disabling the opposing agent and removing at least one of its attached blocks, we count this as a rejected submission.

6.2   General Remarks and Improvements

Before diving into the details about the performance of the agents in each match, we would like to first discuss some of the general short-comings that were noticed during review of all simulation replays.

Task Failures. There were a few cases where builders gathered and constructed the requirements for a given task, but missed the deadline within a few steps. This occurred in simulation 3 against LFC (missed 40 points for task14), and simulation 2 against FIT BUT (missed 90 points for task1). In simulation 3 of the LFC match, one of the builders attempted to submit a task outside of a goal cluster. As expected, the submission failed and the master builder ended up dropping the task. This could have been easily prevented by being more thorough with the implementation of the task submission plans. This would ensure an agent is located on a goal space before attempting task submission.

Task Collaboration Bug. The task collaboration bug occurred as a result of an issue with the planning algorithm. This resulted in the master builder not communicating properly with any of the slave builders after the second requirement; this caused both the master and slave builders assigned to the given task to wait indefinitely, or at least until the task became invalid. This would only occur with tasks that had more than 2 requirements. This issue was eventually fixed mid-way through the first simulation of the last team match, and unfortunately cost the agents a lot of points (and matches).

The team struggled to complete tasks in all simulations of the matches against GOAL-DTU and LFC, and the first simulation against FIT BUT. Fortunately, the bug was fixed, and the agents were able to improve their match performance for the last two simulations. This helped the agents score one win, and although they lost their last simulation, they were able to score a large amount of points.

Task Follow-Through. The builders seemed to attach a large amount of blocks from the dispensers, but did not connect or submit these attachments as part of a task. This implies that the builders wasted a lot of time dispensing and attaching blocks just to detach them later on. This premature detachment of blocks resulted from various things, including the inability of slave builders to line up with the task master due to blocked paths, and exceeding task deadlines and being assigned a new task, among other things.

The underlying reason for this is that the agents typically detach a block if they are stuck or in a bad state. Anything that results in this state, including getting stuck in a crowded area or failing an action too many times can trigger the agent to reset itself back to a known state, which includes detaching any blocks. A better way to approach this would be to have a higher tolerance for failure before resetting the state, or to improve detection and understanding of the current surroundings. For example, we can account for agent density in an area and attempt to force movement through the usage of the clear action before requiring a state reset.

Late Task Start Time. For the majority of the matches, the first requirement of the first task was not attached to the agent until about half-way through the match. This metric shows how long it takes for the builders to explore the map and identify each other before they are assigned a task by the operator. Although this is heavily influenced by map size and initial placement of the agents, the agents did not get started on any tasks until around step 217 on average.

The Attacker Agents. The attacker agents will be evaluated based off of the number of opposing task submissions they reject or interrupt. The attacker agents did not have any coordination strategy, and as a result some of the attackers—in some cases, all of the attackers—would monitor the same empty goal cluster. In these cases, we have agents that are essentially sitting at a goal cluster and doing nothing at all.

In the cases where the attacker agents do interrupt any opposing agents, the number of submission rejections is very low. In the best case scenario (simulation 3 against FIT BUT), the attackers were able to reject 5 task submissions. In most simulations, the combined rejection rate of all of the attackers is at most 1 task rejection. The performance of the attackers was extremely poor.

In retrospect, not much time was put into the attacker strategy. It would have been smarter to either assign a smaller portion of the team to attackers, to just get rid of them completely, or to have all agents be builders and allow them to dynamically switch their role to an attacker when they are not busy with any tasks.

6.3   Match Performance Results

The match performance of the TRG team is analyzed in detail utilizing the previously defined match performance metrics. Each match will be discussed briefly, and will be accompanied with a table demonstrating the results of each simulation with respect to the metrics.

Each of the simulation column headings will be colour-coded to dictate whether or not the TRG team won (green), tied (yellow), or lost (red), the corresponding simulation. Task metrics will be greyed out if they are not applicable to the simulation—meaning the builders did not submit any tasks.

Match 1 Performance (vs. GOAL-DTU). TRG struggled to submit tasks in all three simulations against GOAL-DTU. After reviewing the replays, the builders seemed to struggle with block delivery and navigating to their meeting points after gathering their respective requirements. This left the builder agents wandering around the map with attached blocks until their tasks expired. Although the attacker agents were able to reject a few submissions from the other team, it was not enough to compensate for the poor performance of the builders.

The builders were able to submit a total of 1 task with 2 requirements across all 3 simulations. This scored us a grand total of 40 points against GOAL-DTU, who was able to score a total of 120 points. The metrics for this match can be seen in Table 1.

Table 1. The agent metrics for simulations 1–3 against GOAL-DTU. All time metric values are provided in steps.

Metrics (vs. GOAL-DTU)	Simulation 1	Simulation 2	Simulation 3
Score (GOAL-DTU - TRG)	40 - 40	40 - 0	40 - 0
Attachment Utilization (Used/Obtained)	2 / 27	0 / 29	0 / 33
Number of Connections Made	1	0	0
Submitted Tasks	1	0	0
Failed Submissions	0	0	0
First Task Start Time	253		
Avg. Task Requirement Size	2		
Avg. Task Completion Time (Per Req.)	40		
Avg. Attach to Connect Time	72		
Avg. Last Connect to Submit Time	2		
Opponent Rejected Submissions	2	3	1

Match 2 Performance (vs. LFC). Our agents were able to perform marginally better in the second match against LFC. Although the builder agents finally got their act together and starting building tasks correctly, they unfortunately were not able to meet a few of the task deadlines, resulting in failed submissions. On top of this, the builders also struggled to build any tasks that had more than 2 requirements. This was a direct result of the task collaboration bug.

It is safe to say that the attacker agents were completely useless in all three simulations, rejecting a total of 1 submission from the other team. This match could have benefited from less attackers and more builders. The final score across all three simulations was 390 (LFC) - 160 (TRG). The metrics for the match against LFC can be seen in Table 2.

Table 2. The agent metrics for simulations 1–3 against LFC. All time metric values are provided in steps.

Metrics (vs. LFC)	Simulation 1	Simulation 2	Simulation 3
Score (LFC - TRG)	180 - 120	0 - 0	210 - 40
Attachment Utilization (Used/Obtained)	6 / 26	0 / 20	2 / 23
Number of Connections Made	3	1	4
Submitted Tasks	3	0	1
Failed Submissions	0	1	2
First Task Start Time	225		326
Avg. Task Requirement Size	2		2
Avg. Task Completion Time (Per Req.)	19.2		16
Avg. Attach to Connect Time	25.7		21
Avg. Last Connect to Submit Time	2		2
Opponent Rejected Submissions	0	0	1

Match 3 Performance (vs. FIT BUT). After finally tracking down the task collaboration bug mid-way through simulation 1, the builders were able to significantly improve their task performance in the two remaining simulations. TRG secured their first (and only) win in the second simulation against FIT BUT. In the simulation, the builders were able secure the win by submitting 4 tasks, including a task with 3 requirements.

Unfortunately, the same can not be said about the attackers. Their performance was abysmal in the first two simulations, and although they made a small impact in simulation 3, it was not enough to prevent FIT BUT from scoring 500 points in the simulation. The total score across all 3 simulations was 660 (FIT BUT) - 390 (TRG). The metrics for the match against FIT BUT can be seen in Table 3.

Table 3. The agent metrics for simulations 1–3 against FIT BUT. All time metric values are provided in steps.

Metrics (vs. FIT BUT)	Simulation 1	Simulation 2	Simulation 3
Score (FIT BUT - TRG)	80 - 0	80 - 210	500 - 180
Attachment Utilization (Used/Obtained)	0 / 26	9 / 29	6 / 43
Number of Connections Made	1	6	4
Submitted Tasks	0	4	2
Failed Submissions	1	1	0
First Task Start Time		112	167
Avg. Task Requirement Size		2.25	3
Avg. Task Completion Time (Per Req.)		27.2	23.7
Avg. Attach to Connect Time		49.5	37.3
Avg. Last Connect to Submit Time		2	2
Opponent Rejected Submissions	0	0	5

7   Conclusion

This paper presented the approach taken by the TRG agents, detailing the design and implementation of the agents, and the system architecture that provides the backbone for reliable reasoning and behaviour within the competition. The high-level system components that are implemented in Java provide information processing abilities that abstract away from the agents and the AgentSpeak code. The agents access these components through the usage of internal actions and rely on them to provide a useful representation so that the agents may fulfill their intentions as reliably and as accurately as possible.

The high-level system components, which includes the navigation system, the agent identification system, and the requirement planner, among others, all work together to help each agent achieve their respective goals (such as attacking the opposing team, task requirement gathering, collaboration with other team agents, and task submission). The agents are assigned one of two roles and communicate with a centralized agent—the operator—who coordinates the identification of agents, and assigns tasks to builder agents so that they may work together and complete tasks in the simulation.

This paper also presented the various debugging challenges that were faced during the course of agent development. Various approaches were taken in order to improve the overall agent debugging experience. The best approach was to use a combination of the various tools available for debugging, which includes the custom-developed visualization tool, IntelliJ IDE support, and the Jason-provided agent mind inspector. These tools all provide differing levels of information about the agents, and combining their usage with one another provided the most informative and efficient debugging approach.

Every aspect of agent development brought on new and interesting challenges. As we attacked each challenge, and watched the system and agent behaviour evolve, we also re-evaluated the purpose of each system component, as well as the system as a whole. We went through various iterations of strategy and system design which eventually led up to the multi-agent system detailed in this paper.

Considering the challenges we faced during design and development of the agents, and during the competition, we were very happy with the performance of the agents. Even though the team performed poorly overall in the contest, it was very fulfilling to witness the system's components and the agent behaviour work together as they competed against other agents. Although the attacker agents were basically useless, and we could have performed better with a team full of builders, it was still interesting and fun to develop a strategy for the attackers just to see how they would affect the other teams.

We will briefly discuss the limitations of our multi-agent system, and any future work that needs to be done. The agent visualization tool that was created for the purpose of the TRG agents is tightly-coupled to the structure of the agent containers. Improvements to the visualization tool would be to provide a generic interface available to any agent. This would allow the visualization tool to be used by any multi-agent system, and could ideally improve the process of debugging agents for other developers. Additional work could be done to integrate this tool with the Jason mind inspector.

Our multi-agent system also has the drawback of having design components that are tightly-coupled to the MAPC scenario. For example, the agent container and the parsed percept objects are all derived from scenario-specific concepts and challenges. Further work needs to be done on this aspect of the system to generalize these components. These components are meant to handle challenges specific to the MAPC scenario, but if generalized, could be applied to address similar design concerns and challenges faced by other multi-agent systems.

In terms of team strategy, further work could be done to mitigate some of the shortcomings faced during the competition. The attacker role would be reconsidered to minimize the loss of potential task submissions due to an ineffective attacking strategy. The builder role could also be further improved by having multiple master builders within a task sub-team. This allows the builders to work on subsections of the assigned task. This results in a decentralized approach to task building, and would significantly reduce the amount of time that the builders spend waiting for each slave to connect with a single master.

Regarding the scalability of our system, our approach is highly centralized and may fall apart when the team and task sizes get extremely large. Future work in the lens of scalability would include moving to a more decentralized approach. This would require re-thinking the approach taken and could potentially involve removing the need for the operator agent and changing the way the agents coordinate on the tasks (i.e. straying away from the concept of relying on master and slave builders). Additional work may need to be done to decentralize the Java components, however, they have been designed to be as modular and as decoupled as possible making the process of decentralizing these components relatively easy.

We hope our design, debugging, and implementation endeavours can help provide some insight into some of the problems that other multi-agent systems face. As a final note, we would like to thank the MAPC organizers for hosting the competition, and for providing such a challenging, yet fulfilling, scenario for our team.

8   Team Overview: Short Answers

8.1   Participants and Their Background

What was your motivation to participate in the contest? The main motivation was to use the simulation as a concrete example for a thesis topic; while also allowing us to explore the benefits and limitations of Jason.

What is the history of your group? (course project, thesis, ...) Babak is Michael's thesis supervisor. He has helped tremendously with regards to the development of the agents, and the paper.

What is your field of research? Which work therein is related? We aim to explore the intersection of multi-agent systems and epistemic logic. This contest provides many challenges that could be approached with epistemic logic. Although this was not attempted during the contest, we plan on using the simulation as a means for researching the formulation of (and potential solution to) these challenges using epistemic logic.

8.2   Statistics

How much time did you invest in the contest (for programming, organizing your group, other)? An average of 40–50 h a week was spent programming from mid-July to October. No time was spent organizing the group.

How many lines of code did you produce for your final agent team? Total AgentSpeak LOC: 2309 Total Java LOC: 7385

How many people were involved? Only one of the authors (Michael) was directly involved in the agent programming; although weekly meetings were made with Babak as he was able to provide some higher-level direction regarding some of the challenges that were faced in this contest. Babak also helped immensely with regards to the structuring and revision of the content in this paper.

When did you start working on your agents? Agent development started in May 2019. Initially, it involved just playing around with the simulator and attempting to understand the "Agents Assemble" scenario. Serious agent development did not start until mid-July; continuing until the contest in October.

8.3   Agent System Details

How does the team work together? (i.e. coordination, information sharing, ...) How decentralized is your approach? The team works together through both information sharing and coordination. The agents are able to share perceived map information with each other. Agents who are assigned to the same task will coordinate and synchronize with one another, when it is necessary to connect the requirements. There is an external agent, referred to as the operator. The operator does not participate directly in the simulation, but rather exists as a central location for processing team information and notifications. In general, the agents operate independently of each other until it is necessary to coordinate.

Do your agents make use of the following features: Planning, Learning, Organizations, Norms? If so, please elaborate briefly. The agents plan the task requirements using an in-house algorithm that follows the task generation algorithm of the simulation server. In terms of organization, there are two main roles that an agent may take on, which directly influences the behaviour of the agent.

Can your agents change their behaviour during runtime? If so, what triggers the changes? The behaviour of an agent depends on the designated role, and the current state of the agent. The role of an agent is completely static and does not change during runtime. However, an agent that has the responsibility of completing tasks may change its behaviour depending on what the current goal is (obtaining blocks, navigating, exploring, etc.).

Did you have to make changes to the team (e.g. fix critical bugs) during the contest? Yes, I had discovered an issue with the planning algorithm; this resulted in the agents not connecting the blocks properly. Unfortunately, this issue was fixed too late into the simulation.

How did you go about debugging your system? Debugging the behaviour of the agents was the most difficult and time-consuming aspect of the competition. A lot of effort was made to ease the process of debugging, and I found myself relying on Java (especially the internal actions) to compensate for my lack of Jason knowledge and understanding. Jason does come equipped with the agent mind inspector, although I found that I commonly encountered the observer effect while attempting to debug the behaviour of the agents. In order to make the debugging process as painless as possible, we combined the usage of the mind inspector with IDE breakpoints, and a custom-designed visualization tool.

During the contest you were not allowed to watch the matches. How did you understand what your team of agents was doing? Did this understanding help you to improve your team's performance? Through the usage of the custom-designed agent visualization tool, I was able to partially observe the match. The tool provides a visual representation of the map model shared by the agents, and also provides some debugging information. This tool allowed me to visualize what my own team was doing, but didn't provide much insight about the opposing team.

Did you invest time in making your agents more robust? How? After the initial qualification round, I had spent the next two full weeks rebuilding my agents. Some components were completely rebuilt from the ground-up. One of the main issues I was facing before the rebuild, was the synchronization of the map between the identified agents. Perceptions were being written to the map model incorrectly, and providing incorrect data to the path finding algorithm. Upon careful reconstruction of the code base, the agents were able to correctly read and update the shared map model. The rebuilding of the system led to the system design detailed in this paper.

8.4   Scenario and Strategy

What is the main strategy of your agent team? The main strategy of the team is split between two roles. The attackers, which is composed of half of the team, are responsible for chasing down any opponents and using the clear action to destroy any of their blocks.

The other half of the team is composed of the builder agents who aim to complete tasks. The builders will explore the map, until they are assigned a task and requirement by the operator agent. Once they are assigned a task and a requirement, they obtain the required block from a dispenser, and then meet at a designated meeting location. They utilize the connect action to connect their block requirements, and then submit the task. The coordination and building of task requirements is done by a master builder.

There is also an operator agent who is responsible for centralized processing of team information.

Your agents only got local perceptions of the whole scenario. Did your agents try to build a global view of the scenario for a specific purpose? If so, describe it briefly.

Yes, the agents maintained and shared information contained within their respective map models. Each agent's map model is built using the map perceptions the agent receives at the start of every step. The agents can request information from this map model.

How do your agents decide which tasks to complete?

In order for the agents to communicate and collaborate, they must first identify each other. Once a set of agents are identified by one another, they are then able to collaborate on a task. The agents are then assigned a task based on the number of agents in the identified set (the sub-team), the number of requirements needed, and the deadline. The agents prioritize tasks with a higher number of requirements and a further deadline.

Do your agents form ad-hoc teams to complete a task? Yes, tasks are assigned to sub-teams. The sub-teams consist of the agents who have mutually identified one another.

Which aspect(s) of the scenario did you find particularly challenging? The most difficult aspect was trying to get the agents to correctly time the connection of blocks, without causing them to block if the connect action didn't go according to plan. The most time-consuming aspect (although, not the most difficult) was working with the limited perception range.

If another developer needs to integrate your techniques into their code (i.e., same programming language tools), how easy is it to make that integration work?

I attempted to design the code base with modifiability and readability in mind, but as the contest got closer these qualities started to become less of a priority. It is quite a large code base, and I attempted to document it as best as I could, so it shouldn't be too difficult to understand what the agents are doing.

8.5   And the Moral of It Is ...

What did you learn from participating in the contest? The contest helped me with learning and understanding the Jason agent environment (including understanding AgentSpeak, using the provided agent debugger, etc.).

What are the strong and weak points of your team? The agents were designed with a lot of contingency plans in mind. In the case of a failed action, or if the current perceptions are different than what the agent would have expected, the agents are able to adjust their current goals so that they can be in a state that allows them to continue on with what they need to be doing. Unfortunately, having a lot of contingency plans drastically increased the size of the code base, and also made the behaviour of the agents very difficult to debug. Another weak point of the team is that they rely heavily on the map model to perform path finding. Although the agents are resilient to unexpected changes in the map, the limited perception range makes it extremely difficult for agents to reliably navigate to certain destinations.

Where did you benefit from your chosen programming language, methodology, tools, and algorithms? I'd say the main benefit that I gained from my choice of language, was the ability to call Java code from Jason (through internal actions) as it helped compensate for my lack of Jason knowledge, also helping immensely with any debugging issues I had.

Which problems did you encounter because of your chosen technologies? The biggest problem I encountered was losing a lot of time due to not being able to efficiently debug any agent behaviour issues.

Did you encounter new problems during the contest? Yes, I discovered a few issues with the task requirement planning algorithm. Although this technically was not a new problem, it was an existing problem that decided to express itself and hinder the performance of the agents during the competition.

Did playing against other agent teams bring about new insights on your own agents? Other than the fact that our team's attacker agents were useless, there wasn't much new insight brought on from the other teams.

What would you improve (wrt. your agents) if you wanted to participate in the same contest a week from now (or next year)?
The one thing I would do to improve my agents is to develop debugging tools from the very beginning. It was difficult to properly trace a bug using the Jason debugging tools, and so I had to develop my own tool to help understand what any of my agents were doing. If I had developed this tool from the start, it would have greatly improved development and debugging efficiency.

Which aspect of your team cost you the most time?
I'd say that debugging unwanted behaviour was the most time-consuming task. Typically, any issues that occurred in my AgentSpeak code took at least 2–3 days to debug and fix. As time went on, the Jason code became more complex, and because of that it was difficult to pin-point the source of a bug.

What can be improved regarding the contest/scenario for next year?
The contest was really well organized and the documentation was done well. It would be nice to have a skip action from the start, as it saves a lot of time, especially while debugging. It would also be convenient if the simulation provided a way to parse the raw percepts from the EnvironmentInterface into percept-specific Java objects.

Why did your team perform as it did? Why did the other teams perform better/worse than you did? I think the main reason for performing poorly in this contest was that I split the team in half. Rather than having half of the team attack the other team, I think I should have dedicated all agents to completing tasks. On top of this, my agents had an issue with planning their requirements during the contest. This caused the agents to drop their blocks prematurely and go back to re-obtain the block through the dispenser. This drastically reduced the number of tasks that were submitted.

References

1. Bordini, R., Hübner, J., Wooldridge, M.: Programming Multi-Agent Systems in AgentSpeak Using Jason, vol. 8 (2007)
2. Rao, A.S.: AgentSpeak(L): BDI agents speak out in a logical computable language. In: Van de Velde, W., Perram, J.W. (eds.) MAAMAW 1996. LNCS, vol. 1038, pp. 42–55. Springer, Heidelberg (1996). https://doi.org/10.1007/BFb0031845

Author Index

Printed in the United States
By Bookmasters